build
your
korean
vocabulary

SUNJEONG SHIN

New York Chicago San Francisco Lisbon London Madrid Mexico City
Milan New Delhi San Juan Seoul Singapore Sydney Toronto

3 4 5 6 7 8 9 10 11 12 13 14 15   QVS/QVS   1 9 8 7 6 5 4

ISBN 978-0-07-174295-5 (book and CD set)
MHID   0-07-174295-6 (book and CD set)

ISBN 978-0-07-174294-8 (book for set)
MHID   0-07-174294-8 (book for set)

Library of Congress Control Number 2010924715

McGraw-Hill books are available at special quantity discounts to use as premiums and sales promotions or for use in corporate training programs. To contact a representative, please e-mail us at bulksales@mcgraw-hill.com.

This book is printed on acid-free paper.

Introduction

Words, words, words! To get ahead in a language, it is important to build up a base of essential vocabulary. The aim of this book is to help you do just that and, moreover, to make the process as efficient and interesting as possible.

ABOUT THIS BOOK AND CD

Each of the 16 topics covers an area of everyday life, and contains:

Core vocabulary: the key words that will help you build a foundation in each topic area.

Further vocabulary: this will supplement the core vocabulary and enhance your command of the language.

Exercises: the purpose of the exercises is to bring the vocabulary to life. They will help you progress from recognizing the words to actually using them, seeing how they relate to each other and making them yours. They start with the most basic words and then increase in sophistication. A final free-style exercise allows you to express yourself using your new vocabulary.

Language tips: these explain small points of grammar and spelling to help you use the words with greater confidence.

Flashcards: an invaluable aid to help you memorize the core vocabulary. You can take the words with you wherever you go.

Audio CD: gives support for pronunciation of the topic vocabulary, using native-speaker voices. See the audio CD face for track details.

Finally, there is a section with **Examination advice**. This section contains tips on how to prepare for examinations and tests. There is also a list of questions and instructions (rubrics) which can appear in public examinations.

You'll find suggestions and tips on using this book on pages 6–7.

Contents

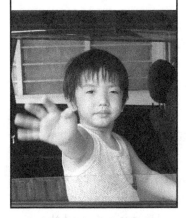

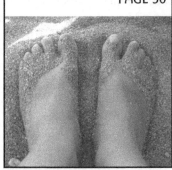

Tear-out section with 640 Korean–English vocabulary flashcards

How to use this book

AS A STUDENT

If you are studying on your own, here is one way of working through the book:

1   Start with the core vocabulary, using the audio CD and flashcards to help you. (Advice on using the flashcards is given below.) Take your time in getting to know these essential words, perhaps over the course of a few days, until you feel comfortable with them.
2   Then take a look at the further vocabulary and phrases. Just try and familiarize yourself with these. There is no need to memorize them.
3   Now it is time to try the exercises. As much as possible, make use of the words you can remember, without looking them up. When you have been through the exercises once, refer back to the lists to see which words you need to review.
4   The final exercises are more open-ended than the others and give you space for personal expression. Feel free to use the words that interest you the most. If you have access to a teacher or a friend who knows Korean, perhaps you can ask them to look over your work and tell you what they think.

If you are attending a course, you can use this book to reinforce and enrich your learning: the word lists and flashcards will give you vocabulary to supplement what you have learned in class; the language tips will highlight and explain the most important grammatical points; the basic exercises will allow you to test your knowledge; and the writing exercises will improve your composition skills.

AS A TEACHER

If you are a teacher, this book is a key classroom tool. Each topic serves as either reinforcement or a point of departure for the study of different aspects of everyday life. The flashcards, exercises and tips can be used to back up and complement the material covered in class, and can also be the basis for classroom activities.

TIPS FOR LEARNING VOCABULARY

1   Relax! You will take in a lot more if you are at ease and having fun.
2   Say the words out loud, mimicking the native-speaker pronunciation on the CD. The vocabulary does not just exist on paper – it is meant to be spoken. Repeat each word over and over so that you feel comfortable saying it.

3 Carry the CD and flashcards around with you. Whenever you have a spare moment, test yourself by playing the CD or by going through a few cards.

4 Use the flashcards as labels, especially for everyday items. Stick them onto the items they refer to so that you associate them with their Korean name.

5 Use the flashcards to store the words in your long-term memory. Here is how:
  • Take five envelopes and label them 1 to 5.
  • Place the flashcards for a topic in envelope 1.
  • Go through the cards and place the words you know into envelope 2 and keep the rest in envelope 1.
  • The next week, go through them again. If you still know a word in envelope 2, move it along to envelope 3. If you know a word from envelope 1, move it along to envelope 2. If you do not know a word, put it back in envelope 1.
  • Each week, do the same, moving the cards to the next envelope if you know the word, or back to envelope 1 if you do not. Keep going until all the words are in envelope 5.

6 Play a memory game. Lay the flashcards for a topic out on a table, with the Korean face up. Choose a card and say the meaning of the word out loud. Then turn the card over to check. If you got the meaning right, you can take the card away. If not, put it back and try another card. Once you can do this, turn all of the cards over and try the same thing, but this time from English into Korean.

7 If you are having difficulty learning a particular word, stick its flashcard onto something you use a lot, such as a refrigerator. Each time you want to use that item, you have to say the word and its meaning before you can go any further!

8 Work with someone else. Test each other on the vocabulary and go through the exercises together. A shared activity can be more enjoyable and motivating.

HOW THE VOCABULARY IS PRESENTED

1 All vocabulary lists are recorded and transliterated to help with pronunciation.

2 Korean nouns do not have grammatical gender, and the singular form is often also used as plural.

3 Adjectives are listed with the polite ending 요 yo.

4 Verbs are generally shown with the infinitive ending 다 da, although occasionally the polite ending 요 yo is included.

Greetings and basics

CORE VOCABULARY

hi *(plain)*	안녕	annyeong.
hello *(informal, honorific)*	안녕하세요?	annyeong-haseyo?
hello *(formal, honorific)*	안녕하십니까?	annyeong-hasimnikka?
bye *(to one leaving/staying, plain)*	잘 가/잘 있어	jal ga/jal isseo
goodbye *(to one leaving/staying, honorific)*	안녕히 가세요/ 안녕히 계세요	annyeonghi gaseyo/ annyeonghi gyeseyo
see you again	또 만나요	tto mannayo
welcome	환영합니다	hwanyeong-hamnida
pleased to meet you	만나서 반갑습니다	mannaseo bangap-seumnida
thank you	고맙습니다/ 감사합니다	gomap-seumnida/ gamsa-hamnida
you're welcome	천만에요	cheonmaneyo
excuse me?	실례합니다	sillye-hamnida
sorry!/excuse me!	죄송합니다!	joesong-hamnida!
yes	네	ne
no	아니오	anio
what?	뭐?	mwo?
who?	누구?	nugu?
where?	어디?	eodi?
when?	언제?	eonje?

how?	어떻게?	eotteoke?
why?	왜?	wae?
which one?	어떤거?	eoddeongeo?
opposite	맞은편	majeun-pyeon
between	사이	sai
toward	향해	hyang-hae
around	주위	juwi
in	안	an
out	밖	bak
above	위	wi
on	위	wi
below	아래	arae
next to	옆	yeop
inside	안쪽	anjjok
outside	바깥쪽	bakkatjjok
I *(plain/polite)*	나 / 저	na/jeo
you *(plain/polite)*	너 / 당신	neo/dangsin
he	그	geu
she	그녀	geu-nyeo
it	그것	geu-geot
we	우리	uri
they	그들	geu-deul

FURTHER VOCABULARY

good night *(plain/honorific)*	잘 자/ 안녕히 주무세요	jal ja/ annyeonghi jumuseyo
see you tomorrow	내일 만나요	naeil mannayo
sorry *(for the inconvenience)*	미안합니다	mian-hamnida
no problem	문제 없어요	munje eobsseoyo

help!	도와 주세요!	dowa juseyo!
have a good day	좋은 하루 되세요	joeun haru doeseyo
have a good time	좋은 시간 되세요	joeun sigan doeseyo
send my regards	안부 전해주세요	anbu jeonhae-juseyo
happy birthday	생일축하합니다	saengil chukha-hamnida
Autumn Harvest Festival	추석	chuseok
Korean New Year's Day	설날	seolnal
Christmas	성탄절	seongtan-jeol
Easter	부활절	buhwal-jeol
that's good	좋아요	joayo
that's right	맞아요	majayo

 # USEFUL PHRASES

My name is...	제 이름은...
What's your name?	이름이 뭐예요?
Where are you from?	어디에서 왔어요?
I'm from the United States.	저는 미국에서 왔어요.
How have you been? *(formal)*	어떻게 지내셨어요?
How have you been? *(informal)*	잘 지냈어요?
I've been well.	저는 잘 지냈어요.
I'm fine.	저는 잘 지내요.

 ## REMEMBER

The pronouns 당신 (you), 그/그녀 (he/she), etc. are not generally used in conversation, as the context usually makes the subject clear. When talking about yourself, you can either use or omit 저 *(I)*: 저는 잘 지냈어요 *(I've been well)* or just 잘 지냈어요 *(have been well)*.

The pronouns are, however, often used in written Korean.

1. Look at the pictures and decide what the people are saying to each other, choosing from the expressions in the box below, as in the example.

1 안녕히 주무세요.

2 고맙습니다.

3 안녕하세요.

4 천만에요.

5 환영합니다.

2. Match the Korean pronouns to the English, as in the example.

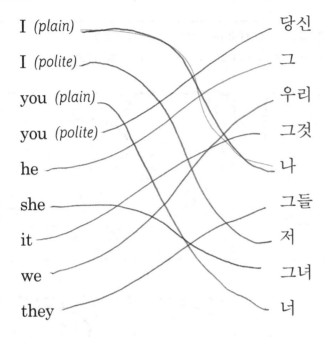

I (plain)	당신
I (polite)	그
you (plain)	우리
you (polite)	그것
he	나
she	그들
it	저
we	그녀
they	너

3. Use an appropriate preposition (in, on, etc.) to say where the cat (고양이 goyangi) is in relation to the car (차 cha).

I 고양이가 차 <u>위</u> 에 있어요.

2 고양이가 차 <u>안</u> 에 있어요.

3 고양이가 차 <u>아래</u> 에 있어요.

4 고양이가 차 <u>옆</u> 에 있어요.

4. You are sending a card to your friend, Minjun, on his birthday. Write a brief message, using phrases from the list. Some of the words are given as clues.

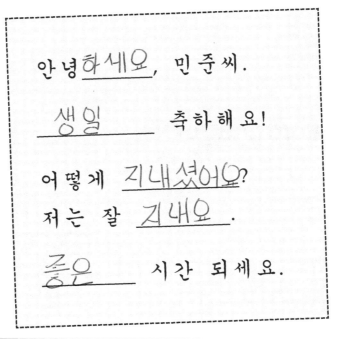

안녕하세요, 민준 씨.

생일   축하해요!

어떻게 지내셨어요?
저는 잘 지내요.

좋은   시간 되세요.

 REMEMBER

In Korean there are three form expressing tiers of politeness; honorific, polite and plain. All of the forms are shown in verb endings. Between friends or to children, the plain form is used, omitting the verb endings altogether: 만나 manna *(meet)*; to someone older or superior, the honorific form is used: 만나세요 mannaseyo; otherwise, the polite ending is mostly used in conversation: 만나요 mannayo.

There is no direct equivalent of *good morning, good afternoon*, etc; the phrases for *hi/hello* (안녕, 안녕하세요 and 안녕하십니까) are used at all times. However, when saying good-bye there is a phrase spoken by the person who is staying and a different phrase spoken by the person who is leaving (see page 10).

House and home

CORE VOCABULARY

live, reside	살아요	sarayo
house	집	jib
apartment	아파트	apateu
villa	빌라	bila
apartment building	아파트 단지	apateu danji
district, area	지역	jiyeok
street	거리	geori
small	작아요	jagayo
big, large	커요	keoyo
old	낡았어요	nalgasseoyo
modern	현대적이에요	hyeondaejeo-gieyo
quiet	조용해요	joyong-haeyo
crowded	복잡해요	bokjap-haeyo
comfortable	편안해요	pyeonan-haeyo
furnished	가구가 달렸어요	gaguga dallyeosseoyo
floor *(level)*	층	cheung
lift, elevator	승강기	seung-gang-gi
room	방	bang
bedroom	침실	chimsil
living room	거실	geosil
dining room	식당	sikdang

office, study	공부방	gongbubang
kitchen	부엌	bu-eok
bathroom	욕실	yoksil
garden	정원	jeongwon
carpet	카페트	kapeteu
curtain	커튼	keoteun
sofa	소파	sopa
bed	침대	chimdae
oven	오븐	obeun
refrigerator	냉장고	naengjang-go
table	상	sang
chair	의자	uija
door	문	mun
window	창문	changmun
bell	종	jong
air-conditioning	에어콘	e-eokon
toilet	화장실	hwajangsil
rent	임차	imcha
to rent	임대	imdae

FURTHER VOCABULARY

reception room	응접실	eung-jeop-sil
hall, reception area	현관	hyeon-gwan
stairs, ladder	계단	gyedan
garage	창고	chang-go
swimming pool	수영장	suyeongjang
furniture	가구	gagu
place, locality	장소	jangso
agency	대리점	daerijeom

for sale	세일	seil
parking space	주차 구역	jucha-guyeok
it is situated (in)	위치해 있다	wichihae idda
to move house	이사해요	isahaeyo

 USEFUL PHRASES

The ground floor consists of the kitchen, dining room and living room.	일층에 부엌과 식당과 거실이 있어요.
I live in an apartment on the first floor of a large apartment building.	저는 큰 아파트 단지 안의 아파트 일층에 살아요.
My house is situated in Gang-Nam	저희 집은 강남에 위치해 있어요.
I'd like to rent a furnished apartment.	가구가 달린 아파트를 임대하고 싶어요.
My room is small but it's comfortable.	제 방은 작아요. 하지만 편안해요.

 REMEMBER

Korean is a syllabic language with 14 basic consonants and 10 basic vowels. The letters are written in squares. Each square makes up a single syllable with combinations of at least one consonant and one vowel. See the examples below. (The letter ㅇ is used to "carry" an opening vowel.)

ㄱ + ㅏ = 가 (ga)

ㄴ + ㅓ + ㅁ = 넘 (neom)

ㅇ + ㅏ + ㄴ + ㅈ = 앉 (anj)

Koreans often use the word 우리 uri ("our") in place of "my." For example:

This is my ("our") house.	우리 집이에요.
My ("our") mom is coming.	우리 엄마가 와요.

EXERCISES

I. Complete the crossword using the Korean equivalents of the words in the list. Write a syllable in each square.

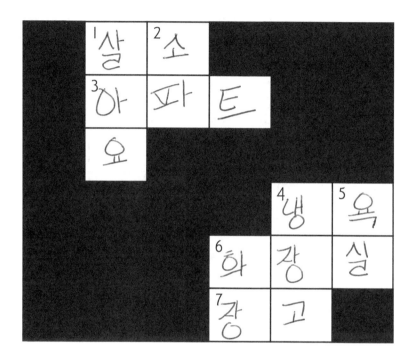

Across

3 apartment 아파트

6 toilet 화장실

7 garage 창고

Down

I live 살아요

2 sofa 소파

4 refrigerator 냉장고

5 bathroom 욕실

2. Label the pictures with the appropriate adjective in the box below.

3 조용해요
  quiet

2 낡았어요
  large _old._

3 현대적이에요
  modern

4 복잡해요
  crowded

3. Translate the sentences below.

a The house is large.

집이 커요

b The villa is old.

빌라가 낡았어요

c The elevator is crowded.

승강기가 복잡해요

d The apartment is furnished.

e The room is comfortable.

4. Label the rooms in the house, using the words in the box.

Label	Word

5 욕실

3 침실

4 거실

1 부억

2 정원

Box words:
1 부억
2 정원
3 침실
4 거실
5 욕실

5. Write 3–4 sentences about your home. Include details such as:

● whether it's a house or an apartment (how many floors?)

● a short description (quiet? comfortable? large?, etc.)

● one or two details about the individual rooms

Family and friends

![] CORE VOCABULARY

family	가족	gajok
relative	친척	chincheok
father	아버지	abeoji
mother	어머니	eomeoni
parents	부모님	bumonim
older brother *(to a female/to a male)*	오빠 / 형	oppa/hyeong
younger brother	남동생	nam-dongsaeng
older sister *(to a female/to a male)*	언니 / 누나	eonni/nuna
younger sister	여동생	yeo-dongsaeng
son	아들	adeul
daughter	딸	ttal
wife	아내	anae
husband	남편	nampyeon
boy	남자애	namja-ae
girl	여자애	yeoja-ae
uncle *(paternal/maternal)*	삼촌 / 외삼촌	samchon/oe-samchon
aunt *(paternal/maternal)*	고모 / 이모	gomo/imo
cousin *(paternal/maternal)*	사촌 / 외사촌	sachon/eo-sachon
grandfather *(paternal/maternal)*	할아버지 / 외할아버지	harabeoji/eo-harabeoji

grandmother (*paternal/maternal*)	할머니 / 외할머니	halmeoni/eo-halmeoni
grandson	손자	sonja
granddaughter	손녀	sonnyeo
nephew, niece	조카	joka
bride	신부	sinbu
bridegroom	신랑	sinlang
married	결혼했어요	gyeorhon-haesseoyo
marriage	결혼	gyeorhon
divorced	이혼했어요	ihon-haesseoyo
divorce	이혼	ihon
single (*m*)	총각	chonggak
single (*f*)	처녀	cheonyeo
child	어린이	eorini
baby	아기	agi
man	남자	namja
woman	여자	yeoja
youth	청년	cheongnyeon
friend	친구	chingu
was born	태어났어요	taeeonasseoyo
died (*plain/honorific*)	죽었어요 / 돌아가셨어요	jugeosseoyo/ doragasyeosseoyo
get married (I)	결혼해요	gyeorhonhaeyo

FURTHER VOCABULARY

members of the family	식구	sikgu
fiancé	약혼자	yakhon-ja
fiancée	약혼녀	yakhon-nyeo
separated	별거해요	byeolgeohaeyo
twin	쌍둥이	ssangdung-i
adult	어른	eoreun

mother-in-law *(to a female/to a male)*	시어머니/장모님	si-eomeoni, jangmonim
father-in-law *(to a female/to a male)*	시아버지/장인어른	si-abeoji, jangin-eoreun
adolescent	청소년	cheongsonyeon
young woman	아가씨	agassi
orphan	고아	goa
widower	홀아비	horabi
widow	과부	gwabu
widowed	사별했어요	sabyeolhaesseoyo
the elderly	노인	noin
to introduce	소개하다	sogaehada
to first meet	처음 만나다	cheoeum mannada
to bring up	키우다	kiwuda
to adopt	입양하다	ibyanghada

 # USEFUL PHRASES

Who's this?	누구예요?
This is my friend, MiJin.	제 친구, 미진이에요.
This is my younger brother, JinSu.	제 남동생, 진수예요.
Pleased to meet you.	만나서 반갑습니다.
My friend's name is SuYeon.	제 친구 이름은 수연이에요.
I was born in Seoul.	저는 서울에서 태어났어요.
My mother was born in the year ...	우리 어머니는 ... 에 태어났어요.
My grandfather died last year.	우리 할아버지는 작년에 돌아가셨어요.
I first met my friend Sara at school.	학교에서 제 친구 사라를 처음 만났어요.

EXERCISES

1. How many of the words from the list can you find?

가	남	해	주	요	제	사	미
족	람	총	각	남	아	친	영
진	가	마	소	낭	포	구	배
유	진	어	가	고	남	이	새
로	찬	린	부	머	자	나	모
종	과	이	거	국	애	일	행
본	라	음	모	비	잔	우	마
세	타	건	어	머	니	수	벼
여	대	남	악	학	이	주	방
남	편	포	소	기	여	자	애

family

girl

boy

friend

husband

mother

child

single *(m)*

2. Fill in the gaps in the family tree, as in the example.

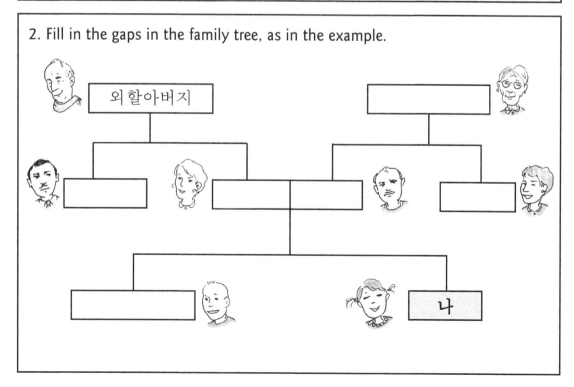

외할아버지

나

3. Fill the boxes with synonyms (words with the same meaning) or near-synonyms (words with a similar meaning).

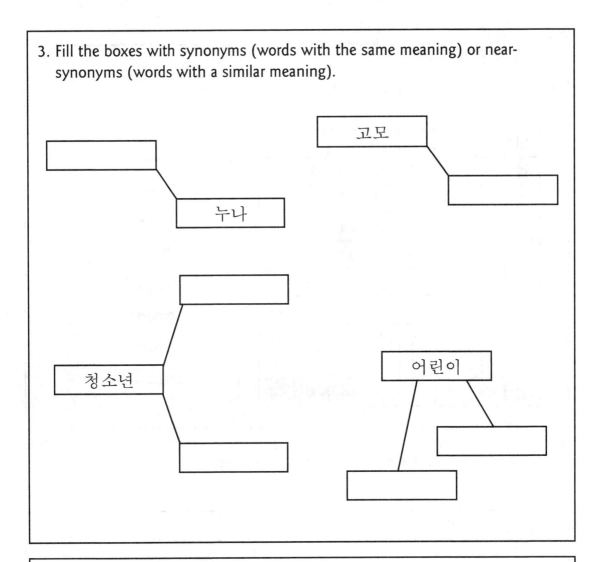

4. Complete the following sentences.

1 제 친구 남편이 죽었어요. 제 친구는 _____ 예요.

2 우리 여동생이 9월에 결혼해요. _____ 을 대학교에서 만났어요.

3 우리 어머니는 언니가 둘, 동생이 하나예요. 그래서 저는
_____ 가 세 명이에요.

4 저는 _____ 가 넷이에요. 딸 셋 그리고 아들 하나예요.

5. Write 4–5 sentences about your family and friends. Include details such as:

- how many brothers and sisters or children you have (+ names)
- where and when you and other family members were born
- the name(s) of friend(s) and where you met them

_____

_____

_____

_____

_____

 REMEMBER

There are different words for older sister or older brother depending on whether the speaker is male or female. For males, older sister is 누나 nuna and older brother 형 hyeong. For females, older sister is 언니 eonni and older brother 오빠 oppa. For relatives on the maternal side, prefix 외 eo is added to indicate the difference.

To talk about possession in Korean, we often use 의 ui (of) between the two nouns, but this can be omitted. For example:

This is my sister's room. 제 언니의 방이에요. **or** 제 언니 방이에요.

This is my friend's mother. 제 친구의 어머니예요. **or** 제 친구 어머니예요.

Verb infinitives in Korean always end with 다 da, e.g. 만나다 mannada _(to meet)_, 가다 gada _(to go)_. The ending changes when a verb is put in a sentence. For example, the polite present tense ending is 요 yo, giving 만나요 mannayo and 가요 gayo. The honorific equivalent is 세요 seyo, giving 만나세요 mannaseyo and 가세요 gaseyo. (See also page 13.)

Character and feelings

CORE VOCABULARY

personality, character	성격	seonggyeok
characteristic	개성	gaeseong
feelings	감정	gamjeong
temperament	성질	seongjil
(good) manners	매너 있어요	maneo isseoyo
nice	좋아요	joayo
happy	행복해요	haengbokhaeyo
sad	슬퍼요	seulpeoyo
truthful	진실해요	jinsilhaeyo
sorry	유감스러워요	yugamseureowoyo
funny	웃겨요	utgyeoyo
distressing	괴로워요	goerowoyo
exciting	흥미로워요	heungmirowoyo
amazing	놀라워요	nollawoyo
different	달라요	dallayo
similar	비슷해요	biseuthaeyo
strange	이상해요	isanghaeyo
normal, usual	늘 마찬가지예요	neul machangajiyeyo
boring	지루해요	jiruhaeyo
strong	튼튼해요	teunteunhaeyo
weak	약해요	yakhaeyo
angry	화났어요	hwa-nasseoyo

shy	수줍워요	sujubeoyo
generous	관대해요	gwandaehaeyo
miserly	인색해요	insaekhaeyo
clever	똑똑해요	ttokttokhaeyo
stupid	멍청해요	meongcheonghaeyo
lazy	게을러요	ge-eulleoyo
energetic	활동적이에요	hwaldongjeogiyeyo
well-behaved	착해요	chakheyo
afraid (of)	두려워해요	duryeowohaeyo
joyful	즐거워요	jeulgeowoyo
very	매우, 아주	maeu, aju
a little	조금	jogeum
completely	완전히	wanjeonhi
to believe	믿다	mitta
to think	생각하다	saenggakhada
to like	좋아하다	joahada
to dislike, to hate	싫어하다	sireohada
to feel	느끼다	neukkida

FURTHER VOCABULARY

mood	기분	gibun
loyal	충성스러워요	chungseong-seureowoyo
sincere	신실해요	sinsilhaeyo
patient	참을성이 있어요	chameulseongi isseoyo
serious	심각해요	simgakhaeyo
pleased, glad	기뻐요	gippeoyo
hard-working	근면해요	geunmyeonhaeyo
famous	유명해요	yumyeonghaeyo
noisy	시끄러워요	sikkeureowoyo
quiet	조용해요	joyonghaeyo

rudeness, lack of manners	무례함	muryeham
amazement, surprise	놀라움	nollaum
shame	부끄러움	bukkeureoum
disappointment	실망	silmang
loneliness	외로움	woeroum
fear	두려움	dureyoum
excitement	흥분	heungbun
pleasant	유쾌해요	yukoehaeyo
horrible	끔찍해요	kkeumjjikhaeyo
reasonable	이치에 맞아요	ichie majayo
selfish	이기적이에요	igijeogiyeyo
nervous	긴장되요	ginjangdoeyo
honorable	존경스러워요	jongeyongseureowoyo
wise	지혜로워요	jihyerowoyo
brave	용감해요	yonggamhaeyo
to smile	미소짓다	misojitta
to laugh	웃다	utta
to cry	울다	ulda
to lie	거짓말하다	geojitmalhada

 # USEFUL PHRASES

My father is in a good mood today.	우리 아버지는 오늘 기분이 좋아요.
Yesterday he was in a bad mood.	어제 그는 기분이 나빴어요.
I feel lonely.	저는 외로워요.
I was disappointed.	저는 실망했어요.
Patience is a virtue.	참는 자에게 복이 있다.
She was in floods of tears.	그녀는 눈물바다를 만들었어요.
From the cradle to the grave.	요람에서 무덤까지.

EXERCISES

I. Find words from the main vocabulary list to describe the people in the pictures.

1 _____

2 _____

3 _____

4 _____

5 _____

6 _____

2. Write down the opposites of the adjectives below.

1 행복해요 _____

2 튼튼해요 _____

3 시끄러워요 _____

4 지적이에요 _____

5 인색해요 _____

3. From the vocabulary list, put the adjectives into these categories:
- very positive (매우 긍정적)
- positive (긍정적)
- negative (부정적)
- very negative (매우 부정적)

매우 긍정적	긍정적	부정적	매우 부정적

REMEMBER

In Korean, adjectives behave similarly to verbs. The verb is normally placed at the end of a sentence, and likewise adjectives. Look at the examples below.

Verb at the end:

저는 <u>웃어요</u>. *I <u>laugh</u>*.

제 언니는 제 친구와 <u>결혼했어요</u>. *My sister <u>married</u> my friend*.

Adjective at the end:

저는 <u>행복해요</u>. *I'm <u>happy</u>*.

제 동생은 <u>게을러요</u>. *My younger brother is <u>lazy</u>*.

4. Here is a short paragraph in which someone describes the personality of a cousin, Insu:

저는 사촌오빠가 있어요. 그의 이름은 인수예요. 인수오빠는 부산에서 태어났어요. 지금은 서울에서 살아요. 그는 아주 조용해요. 오빠의 긍정적인 성격 중에 하나는 정직한 거예요. 부정적인 성격 중에 하나는 인색한 거예요.

Now write a similar paragraph about someone you know, or a famous person. Use the following phrases to help you:

- his/her name is...   그의/그녀의 이름은 ...이에요

- he/she was born in...   그는/그녀는...에서 태어났어요

- he/she lives in...   그는/그녀는...에 살아요

- among his/her positive   그의/그녀의 긍정적인 성격
  characteristics is that he/she...   중에 하나는 ...거예요.

- among his/her negative   그의/그녀의 부정적인 성격
  characteristics is that he/she...   중에 하나는 ...거예요.

_____

_____

_____

_____

_____

_____

Shopping

CORE VOCABULARY

store	상점	sangjeom
shop	가게	gage
open	열어요	yeoreoyo
closed	닫아요	dadayo
market	시장	sijang
shopping center	쇼핑센터	syoping-senteo
price	가격	gagyeok
cash (*money*)	현금	hyeongeum
money	돈	don
cheap	싸다	ssada
expensive	비싸다	bissada
offer	할인판매	harin-panmae
clerk	점원	jeomwon
merchant	상인	sangin
bakery	제과점	jegwajeom
butcher	정육점	jeongyukjeom
fish seller	생선가게	saengseon-gage
grocer	식료품점	singnyopumjeom
tailor	재단사	jaedansa
jeweler	보석상	boseoksang
wallet	지갑	jigap

bag	가방	gabang
sack, large bag	베낭	benang
copper	구리	guri
silver	은	eun
gold	금	geum
leather	가죽	gajuk
wood	목재	mokjae
free (of charge)	공짜	gongjja
gift	선물	seonmul
few, a little	조금	jogeum
many, much	많이	mani
account, bill	계산서	gyesanseo
receipt	영수증	yeongsujeung
reduction, sale	세일	seil
to pay	지불하다	jibulhada
to buy	사다	sada
to give	주다	juda
to cost	들다	deulda
it is found, located	...에 있다	...e itta

FURTHER VOCABULARY

department	과	gwa
bottle	병	byeong
package	꾸러미	kkureomi
can	깡통	kkangtong
box	상자	sangja
handbag	핸드백	haendeubaek
handmade	수공품	sugongpum
ivory	상아	sanga

check	수표	supyo
travelers' checks	여행자 수표	yeohaengja supyo
credit card	신용카드	sinyong-kadeu
guarantee	보증	bojeung
currency	화폐	hwapye
exchange	환전	hwanjeon
cashier	출납원	chulnabwon
exchange rate	환율	hwanyul
the change	잔돈	jandon
tax	세금	segeum
trader	상인	sangin
traditional	민속의, 전통의	minsogui, jeontongui
natural	자연의	jayeonui
artificial	인공의	ingongui
department store	백화점	baekhwajeom
plastic bag	비닐 봉지	binil bongji
to choose	고르다	goreuda
to exchange *(an item)*	바꾸다	bakkuda
to change *(money)*	환전하다	hwanjeonhada
to agree *(e.g. on a price)*	합의보다	habuiboda

 USEFUL PHRASES

May I help you?	도와 드릴까요?
How much is this?	얼마예요?
When does the store close?	언제 문을 닫아요?
I want a suitable gift for my mother.	어머니께 드릴 선물을 사고 싶은데요.
Is this the final price?	최종가격이에요?
Do you arrange shipping?	배로 보내주나요?

EXERCISES

I. Choose a word from the list below to describe each of the pictures.

재단사	닫아요
가방	생선가게
열어요	병
비싸다	싸다

2. Match the store signs with the activities:

A Have your shirt mended

B Change travelers' checks

C Browse for souvenirs

D Buy a packet of sugar

E Find a bargain

F Buy a ring or bracelet

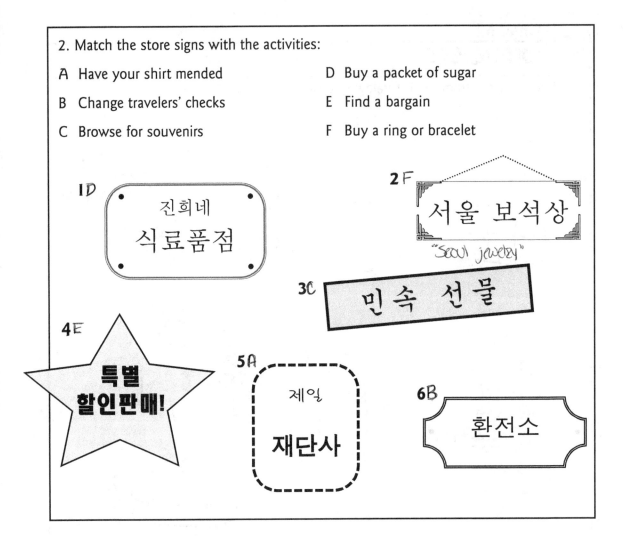

1 D 진희네 식료품점

2 F 서울 보석상 "Seoul jewelry"

3 C 민속 선물

4 E 특별 할인판매!

5 A 제일 재단사

6 B 환전소

3. Circle the odd-one-out in each set of words.

1	금	은	화폐	구리
2	가게	상점	시장	병
3	신용카드	점원	돈	수표
4	가방	비닐 봉지	지갑	백화점

4. Make six sentences about a shopping trip, using the grid below. Notice the order. The first column indicates *when* the action took place; the next shows *who* went; the third shows *where*; the fourth gives the *verb of movement* with the particle 서 indicating intention; the next shows the *items*; and the final column shows *what* was done.

expressions of time	subject (people)	places	verbs of movement and inention	items	shopping verbs
아침에 *(in the morning)*	저는 *(I)*	시장에 *(to the market)*	가서 *(went and)*	...을/를 *(a/some...)*	샀어요. *(bought)*
오후에 *(in the afternoon)*	우리는 *(we)*	은행에 *(to the bank)*		돈을 *(money)*	바꿨어요. *(changed)*
저녁에 *(in the evening)*		상점에 *(to the shop)*		선물을 *(gifts)*	골랐어요. *(chose)*
처음에 *(first)*		식료품점에 *(to the grocery store)*		과일을 *(fruit)*	
그리고 *(then)*		백화점에 *(to a depart-ment store)*			
그리고 나서 *(after that)*					

Example: 아침에 저는 백화점에 가서 가방을 샀어요.

    In the morning I went to a department store and bought a bag.

 REMEMBER

• In Korean there are particles used to indicate the functions of nouns: 이 i, 가 ga, 은 eun, 는 neun after the subject; and 을 eul, 를 reul after the object. When a noun ends with a vowel, 가, 는 or 를 is used. When a noun ends in a consonant 이, 은 or 을 is used. For example:

Subject: 저 (I) + 는 = jeo-neun   서울 (Seoul) + 은 = 서울은 seoul-eun

Object: 돈 (money) + 을 = don-eul   수표 (check) + 를 = 수표를 supyo-reul

TOPIC 6

Clothes and colors

CORE VOCABULARY

clothes	옷	ot
fashion	패션	paesyeon
underwear	속옷	sogok
size	사이즈	saijeu
shirt	셔츠	syeocheu
pants, trousers	바지	baji
shoe	신발	sinbal
sandal	샌달	saendal
jacket	자켓	jaket
suit	정장	jeongjang
dress	드레스	deureseu
skirt	치마	chima
blouse	브라우스	beurauseu
coat	코트	koteu
waistcoat	조끼	jokki
glove	장갑	janggap
sock	양말	yangmal
hat	모자	moja
belt	혁대	hyeottae
jeans	청바지	cheongbaji
bathrobe	드레싱 가운	deuresing gaun

cloth, textile	천	cheon
wool	모직	mojik
cotton	면	myeon
silk	비단	bidan
black (colored)	검정 (색)	geomjeong(saek)
red (colored)	빨강 (색)	ppalgang(saek)
yellow (colored)	노랑 (색)	norang(saek)
blue (colored)	파랑 (색)	parang(saek)
white (colored)	흰 (색)	huin(saek)
green (colored)	녹 (색)	nok(saek)
brown (colored)	갈 (색)	gal(saek)
orange (colored)	주황 (색)	juhwang(saek)
pink (colored)	분홍 (색)	bunhong(saek)
purple (colored)	보라 (색)	bora(saek)
light (colored)	연한 (색)	yeonghan(saek)
dark, deep (colored)	진한 (색)	jinhan(saek)
comfortable	편안하다	pyeonanhada
to wear, to put on	입다	ibtta
to take off	벗다	beotta

FURTHER VOCABULARY

sleeve	소매	somae
collar	칼라	kalla
pocket	주머니	jumeoni
label	상표	sangpyo
sweater	스웨터	seuweteo
raincoat	비옷	biot
uniform	유니폼	yunipom
tie	넥타이	nektai
scarf	목돌이	mokdori

buckle	버클	beokeul
sole	신발 바닥	sinbal-badak
ring	반지	banji
earring	귀걸이	gwigeori
necklace	목걸이	mokgeori
to iron	다림질하다	darimjilhada
to repair	고치다	gochida

 USEFUL PHRASES

These clothes suit you	옷이 잘 어울려요.
What's your size?	사이즈가 뭐예요?
Is this silk/cotton/wool?	이게 비단/면/모직이에요?
I'd prefer the color to be darker/lighter.	더 진한색/연한색 있나요?
"Fine feathers make fine birds."	옷이 날개다.

(Korean saying)

 REMEMBER

"To wear" or "to put on" translates as different verbs in Korean depending on the item:

Items	To wear/to put on	Example sentence
clothes	입다 ibtta	코트를 입어요.
footwear	신다 sinda	신발을 신어요.
headwear	쓰다 sseuda	모자를 써요.
rings, gloves	끼다 kkida	반지를 껴요.
earrings, necklace, scarf, tie, belt	하다 hada	귀걸이를 해요

EXERCISES

I. Find words in the vocabulary list to describe the pictures below.

1 _____

2 _____

3 _____

4 _____

5 _____

6 _____

7 _____

8 _____

2. Circle the odd-one-out in each set of words.

I 코트	장갑	청바지	목걸이
2 바지	셔츠	블라우스	스웨터
3 면	비단	모직	사이즈
4 검정색	파랑색	신발	분홍색

3. SoYeong is a very tidy person. She has a shelf for each type of clothing.

Shelf 1: upper body clothing (blouses, sweaters, etc.)
Shelf 2: lower body clothing (pants, skirts, etc.)
Shelf 3: jewelry
Shelf 4: accessories (hats, scarves, etc.)
Shelf 5: footwear

SoYeong is at work. Her little sister JinJu has just been through her wardrobe and taken all the items out to try them on, but can't remember where everything goes. Can you help JinJu put everything back in the right place before SoYeong gets back?

Write the shelf number next to the item in the box below, as in the example.

바지	**2**	블라우스	☐	장갑	☐	양말	☐
목걸이	☐	반지	☐	치마	☐	청바지	☐
자켓	☐	혁대	☐	신발	☐	샌달	☐
목돌이	☐	모자	☐	스웨터	☐	귀걸이	☐

4. You are about to go clothes shopping for your family . Make 5–6 sentences about what you plan to buy for them. Use the table below to help you.

Subject	For whom	Description (adj)	Clothing	Want to buy
저는 (I)	가족을 위해 (for my family)	예쁜 (pretty)	옷을 (clothes)	사고 싶어요. (want to buy)
	어머니를 위해 (for my mother)	작은 (small)	반지를 (ring)	
	아들을 위해 (for my son)	파랑색 (blue)	넥타이를 (tie)	
	여동생을 위해 (for my sister)	빨강색 (red)	블라우스를 (blouse)	
	아버지를 위해 (for my father)	큰 (big)	코트를 (coat)	
	딸을 위해 (for my daughter)	etc. (see vocabulary list)		

Example: 저는 딸을 위해 빨강색 블라우스를 사고 싶어요.
  I want to buy a red blouse for my daughter.

 REMEMBER

To say "wish to" or "want to," the ending -고 싶어요 -go sipeoyo is added onto the verb stem.

사다 sada *to buy* ➤ 사고 싶어요 sago sipeoyo *want to buy*

가다 gada *to go* ➤ 가고 싶어요 gago sipeoyo *want to go*

Food and drink

CORE VOCABULARY

food	음식	eumsik
menu	메뉴	menyu
dish	반찬	banchan
meal	식사	siksa
sugar	설탕	seoltang
butter	버터	beoteo
salt	소금	sogeum
pepper	후추	huchu
bread	빵	ppang
cooked rice	밥	bap
oil	기름	gireum
cheese	치즈	chijeu
eggs	달걀	dalgyal
meat	고기	gogi
lamb, mutton	양고기	yang-gogi
beef	소고기	sogogi
pork	돼지고기	dwaejigogi
chicken	닭고기	dakgogi
fish	생선	saengseon
vegetables	채소	chaeso
fruit	과일	gwail

salad	샐러드	saelleodeu
soy sauce	간장	ganjang
onions	양파	yangpa
potatoes	감자	gamja
carrots	당근	danggeun
grapes	포도	podo
apples	사과	sagwa
oranges	오렌지	orenji
lemons	레몬	leomon
bananas	바나나	banana
milk	우유	uyu
juice	주스	juseu
water	물	mul
coffee	커피	keopi
tea	차	cha
alcohol	술	sul
dessert, sweet	후식	husik
to eat	먹다	meoktta
to drink	마시다	masida

FURTHER VOCABULARY

can, tin, box	통	tong
canned food	통조림	tongjorim
plate	접시	jeobsi
cooking pot	냄비	naembi
vinegar	식초	sikcho
sausages	소세지	soseji
chocolate	초콜릿	chokollit
mushrooms	버섯	beoseot
cucumbers	오이	oi

figs	무화과	muhwagwa
cherries	체리	cheri
raisins	건포도	geonpodo
pineapple	파인애플	painaepeul
strawberry	딸기	ttalgi
nuts	견과류	gyeongwaryu
vegetarian	채식주의자	chaesik-juuija
fried	볶은음식	bokkeun-eumsik
barbecued, grilled	구운음식	gueun-eumsik
boiled	삶은음식	salmeun-eumsik
drink	음료수	eumlyosu
mineral water	생수	saengsu
cola	코카콜라	kokakola
wine	와인	wain
beer	맥주	maekju
to eat (a meal)	식사를 하다	siksareul hada
to taste	맛을 보다	maseul boda
to have breakfast	아침을 먹다	achimeul meokda
to have lunch	점심을 먹다	jeomsimeul meokda
to have dinner	저녁을 먹다	jeonyeokeul meokda

 # USEFUL PHRASES

"Eat well!"/"Bon appétit!"	맛있게 드세요.
"Health and well-being!"	건강을 위하여!
I'd like a kilo of apples please.	사과 일 키로 주세요.
Tea with milk, please.	차에 우유를 넣어 주세요.
I drink coffee without sugar.	커피 설탕 없이 주세요.

TOPIC 7
EXERCISES

I. Choose a word from the list below to describe each of the pictures.

1

2

3

4

5

6

7

8

생선   주스

닭고기   냄비

커피   빵

당근   차

2. You have just returned from the market (시장) and need to unload the shopping into the refrigerator (냉장고). Put each item from the box below in the right section.

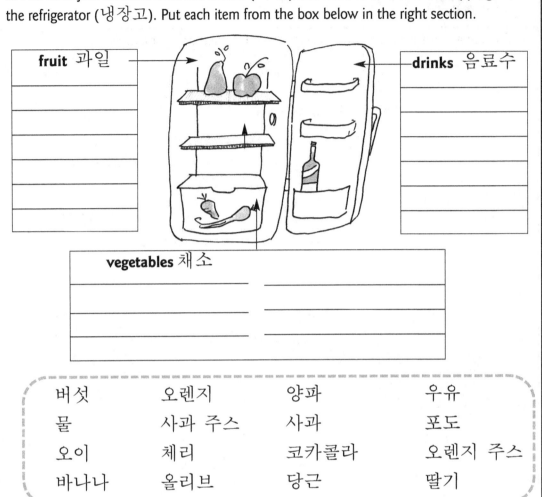

fruit 과일

drinks 음료수

vegetables 채소

버섯	오렌지	양파	우유
물	사과 주스	사과	포도
오이	체리	코카콜라	오렌지 주스
바나나	올리브	당근	딸기

3. Circle the odd-one-out in each set of words.

1	후추	소금	닭고기	기름
2	커피	버터	주스	물
3	메뉴	접시	냄비	깡통
4	당근	올리브	양파	후식

4. Describe your eating habits. You should say what time you have your meals and what you normally eat. Use the tables below to help you.

subject	how often?	time (hour)	time (minute)	meal
저는 (I)	보통 (usually)	일곱 시 (at 7 o'clock)	반에 (half past)	아침을 먹어요. (I have/eat breakfast)
	가끔 (sometimes)	두 시 (at 2 o'clock)	15분에 (15 minutes)	점심을 먹어요. (I have/eat lunch)
	항상 (always)	여섯 시 (at 6 o'clock)	45분에 (45 minutes)	저녁을 먹어요. (I have/eat dinner)

subject	meal	food/drink	eat/drink
저는 (I)	아침에 (for breakfast)	커피를 (coffee)	마셔요. (drink)
	점심에 (for lunch)	샐러드를 (salad)	먹어요. (eat)
	저녁에 (for dinner)	etc. (see vocabulary)	

 REMEMBER

After expressions of time – for example times of the day, dates, meal-times, days of the week, months, etc. – the particle 에 -e is used. This is equivalent to the English prepositions *in, at, on,* and so on.

일곱 시 반에 *at half past seven*

아침에 *in the morning/for breakfast*

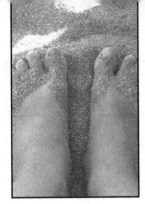

The body

CORE VOCABULARY

body	몸	mom
skeleton	해골	haegol
head	머리	meori
face	얼굴	eolgul
eye	눈	nun
ear	귀	gwi
nose	코	ko
mouth	입	ip
tongue	혀	hyeo
neck	목	mok
belly, stomach	배	bae
arm	팔	pal
leg	다리	dari
foot	발	bal
knee	무릎	mureup
hand	손	son
elbow	팔꿈치	palkkumchi
wrist	손목	sonmok
shoulder	어깨	eokkae
tooth	이빨	ippal

finger	손가락	sonkkarak
toe	발가락	balkkarak
thumb	엄지손가락	eomji sonkkarak
chest	가슴	gaseum
back	등	deung
heart	심장	simjang
hair	머리/머리카락	meori/meorikarak
brain	뇌	noe
blood	피	pi
lung	폐	pye
lip	입술	ibsul
bone	뼈	ppyeo
skin	피부	pibu
to see	보다	boda
to hear	듣다	deutta
to smell	냄새 맡다	naemsae matta
to taste	맛보다	matboda
to touch	만지다	manjida
to move (something)	옮기다	omgida
to move (yourself)	움직이다	umjigida

FURTHER VOCABULARY

muscle	근육	geunyuk
fat	지방	jibang
kidney	신장	sinjang
throat	목구멍	mokgumeong
chin	턱	teok
cheek	볼	bol
eyebrow	눈썹	nunsseop

eyelash	속눈썹	sok-nunsseop
moustache	콧수염	kotsuyeom
beard	수염	suyeom

 USEFUL PHRASES

I have a pain in my leg.	다리가 아파요.
Her hair is long and black.	제 머리는 길고 검어요.
Blood is thicker than water.	피가 물보다 진하다.
In one ear and out the other.	한 귀로 듣고 한 귀로 흘린다.
Walls have ears. ("*The bird hears words in the day and the mouse hears words at night.*")	낮말은 새가 듣고 밤말은 쥐가 듣는다.
The eye is the mirror of the soul. (*Korean saying*)	눈은 마음의 창이다.

 REMEMBER

To say *I have a headache, stomach ache*, etc, the verb 아파요 apayo is used. The part of the body is the subject of the sentence:

머리가 아파요. *I have a headache (literally, "My head hurts.")*

배가 아파요. *I have a stomach ache.*

When using an adverb, place it just before the verb. (Notice that you can usually use the singular word to refer to plural parts of the body in Korean.)

발이 <u>많이</u> 아파요. *My feet hurt <u>a lot</u>.*

눈이 <u>조금</u> 아파요. *My eyes hurt <u>a little</u>.*

1. How many of the words from the list can you find?

가	봉	엄	지	손	가	락
등	주	솜	재	민	신	바
나	책	입	술	기	초	염
눈	치	매	질	손	춘	호
다	재	영	람	가	공	즈
옴	다	새	여	락	토	마
비	리	밀	데	너	직	어
펴	자	아	듬	진	려	호
자	댜	얼	굴	반	사	배
머	리	장	밎	앵	주	차

back

lips

thumb

finger

leg

stomach

head

face

2. Match each sense with the relevant part of the body.

with my...	*I...*
손으로	맛봐요
귀로	봐요
코로	들어요
눈으로	만져요
혀로	냄새맡아요

3. Label the parts of the body, using the vocabulary list to help you.

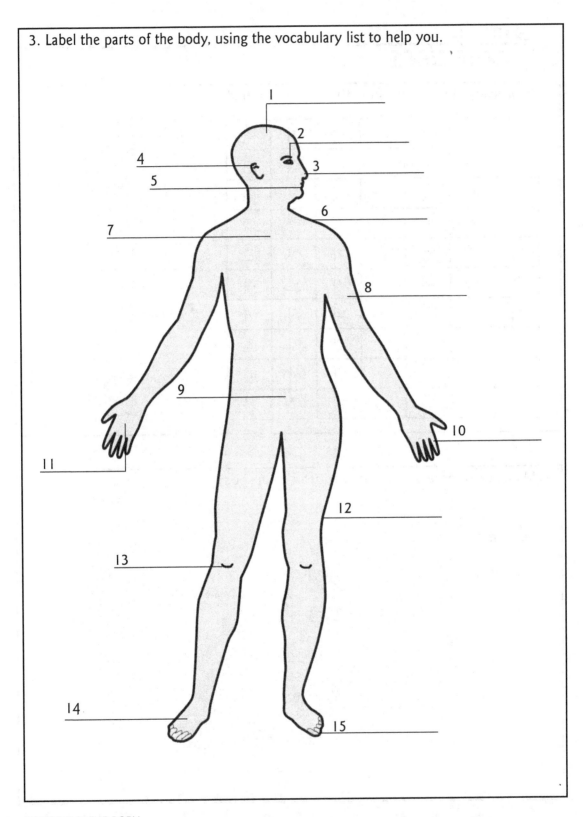

4. Describe yourself or someone you know, based on the table below.

possessive determiner	part of the body (+ subject particle)	adverb	negation (not)	verb-like adjectives
제 (my)	얼굴은 (face)	아주 (very)		예뻐요 (pretty)
당신의 (your)	속눈썹은 (eyelashes)	조금 (a little)		길어요 (long)
그녀의 (her)	코는 (nose)		(안)	작아요 (small)
그의 (his)	머리는 (head)			아름다워요 (beautiful)
	손은 (hand(s))			커요 (big)
	etc. (see vocabulary)			etc. (see vocabulary)

 REMEMBER

To make a sentence negative, add the syllable 안 an (not) before the verb. Note that any adverb will come before 안:

제 속눈썹은 안 길어요. *My eyelashes are not long.*

그의 손은 아주 안 예뻐요. *His hands are not very pretty ("very not pretty").*

Health

CORE VOCABULARY

health	건강	geongang
healthy	건강하다	geonganghada
illness	병	byeong
patient (noun)	환자	hwanja
cold	감기	gamgi
to catch a cold	감기 걸리다	gamgi geollida
sick	아프다	apeuda
fever	열	eol
diarrhea	설사	seolsa
cough	기침	gichim
pulse	맥박	maekbak
headache	두통	dutong
injury	부상	busang
wound	상처	sangcheo
pain	고통	gotong
painful	고통스럽다	gotongseureobda
medicine	약	yak
pill, tablet	알약	alyak
prescription	처방전	cheobangjeon
thermometer	체온계	cheongye
accident	사고	sago

hospital	병원	byeongwon
doctor	의사	uisa
nurse	간호사	ganhosa
ambulance	구급차	gugeubcha
operation, surgery	수술	susul
burn	화상	hwasang
cure, treatment	치료	chiryo
first aid	응급 치료	eunggeub chiryo
habit	습관	seubgwan
addicted (to)	중독되다	jungdokdoeda
smoking	흡연	heubyeon
diet	다이어트	daieoteu
to suffer (from)	고통을 받다	gotongeul batta
to take *(medicine, etc.)*	먹다	meokda
to fall	넘어지다	neomeojida
to break	부러지다	bureojida
to cough	기침하다	gichimhada
to swallow	삼키다	samkida
to smoke	담배피우다	dambaepiuda

FURTHER VOCABULARY

wheelchair	휠체어	hwilche-eo
sunstroke	일사병	ilsabyeong
cancer	암	am
allergy	알레르기	allereugi
diabetes	당뇨	dangnyo
virus	바이러스	baireoseu
influenza	독감	dokgam
chicken pox	수두	sudu

measles	홍역	hongyeok
mumps	이하선염	ihaseonyeom
mental illness	정신병	jeongsinbyeong
stress	스트레스	seuteureseu
bruise	멍	meong
blister	물집	muljib
swelling	부기	bugi
scar	흉터	hyungteo
congested *(nose)*	막히다	makhida
blood pressure	혈압	hyeorap
pregnant	임신하다	imsinhada
to sneeze	재채기하다	jaechaegihada
to gargle	양치질하다	yangchijilhada
to give up *(e.g. smoking)*	끊다	kkeuntta

USEFUL PHRASES

I've had a headache since the morning.	아침부터 머리가 아파요.
What do you have for diarrhea?	설사에 뭐가 좋아요?
Call an ambulance!	구급차를 불러요!
The injury is serious.	부상이 심해요.
I broke my leg.	다리가 부러졌어요.
Is the doctor coming now?	의사가 지금 오고 있나요?
I'm in my fifth month of pregnancy.	임신 오개월째예요.

I. How many of the words from the list below can you find in the word search?

음	중	독	되	다	반	치	뉴	반	담
주	식	설	돼	소	탕	치	메	앤	배
두	지	맥	고	금	고	료	기	싸	피
통	네	박	소	란	주	계	재	름	우
닭	기	생	야	양	기	버	과	그	다
후	미	리	습	관	양	컴	설	사	릇
즈	추	치	선	재	자	터	일	올	당
열	너	어	채	감	파	포	사	기	침
살	러	건	강	하	다	퓨	오	가	참
쥬	드	당	유	나	물	도	바	외	근
고	세	요	감	기	걸	리	다	햐	커
통	래	밤	로	네	어	차	후	피	먹

healthy	to smoke	fever
addicted	treatment	headache
pain	habit	diarrhea
to catch a cold	cough	pulse

2. Find as many words as you can that link to the headings below:

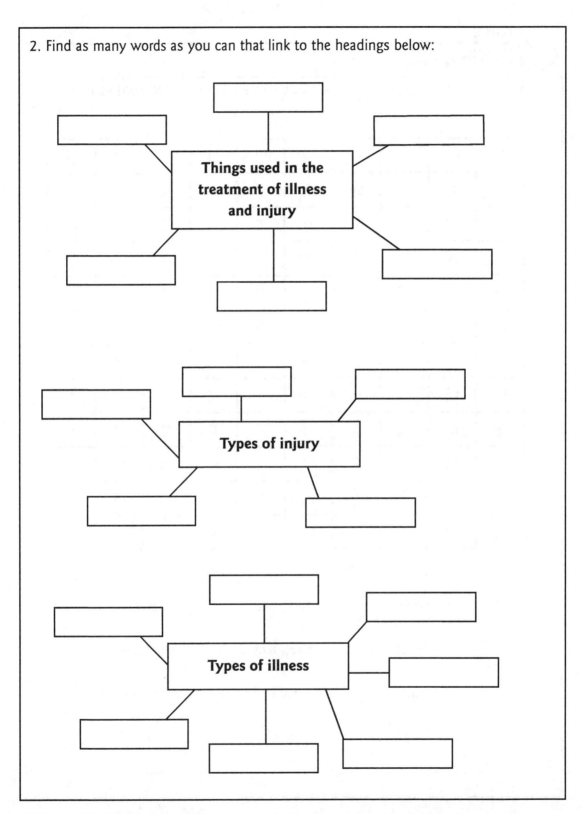

Things used in the treatment of illness and injury

Types of injury

Types of illness

3. Complete the following sentences, using the verbs in the box below.

1 저는 담배를 많이 피워요. 가끔은 하루에 40
개비를 _____.

2 사고 이후에 차 안에만 있으면 스트레스로 _____.

3 밥을 먹은 후에 민주는 배가 _____.

4 기침과 _____를 왜 그렇게 하세요? 감기 걸렸어요?

> 고통을 받아요   재채기
>
> 피워요   아팠어요

REMEMBER

For a question raise your intonation at the end. For a command (*imperative*) your intonation should be almost flat. (Remember that the subject is usually omitted.)

Question

커피 마셔?	Drink coffee? (*plain form*, used among very close friends or when talking to a younger person you know well.)
커피 마셔요?	Would you like to drink coffee? (*polite form*, more casual than the honorific)
커피 마시세요?	Would you like to drink coffee? (*honorific form*)

Command

커피 마셔.	Drink coffee. (*plain form*)
커피 마셔요.	Drink coffee. (*polite form*)
커피 마시세요.	Drink coffee. (*honorific form*)

TOPIC 10
Hobbies

CORE VOCABULARY

hobby	취미	chwimi
spare time	여가 시간	yeoga sigan
sports	운동	undong
athletic	스포티한	seupotihan
game	게임	geim
player	선수	seonsu
team	팀	tim
training	훈련	hullyeon
coach	코치	kochi
soccer, football	축구	chukgu
basketball	농구	nong-gu
volleyball	배구	baegu
tennis	테니스	teniseu
Taekwondo	태권도	taegwondo
Korean wrestling	씨름	ssireum
running, jogging	달리기	dalligi
skiing	스키	seuki
swimming	수영	suyeong
dancing	춤	chum
music	음악	eumak
singing, song	노래	norae

group, band	그룹	geurup
singer	가수	gasu
musical instrument	악기	akgi
flute	플루트	peulluteu
violin	바이올린	baiolin
guitar	기타	gita
piano	피아노	piano
trumpet	트럼펫	teureompet
drum	드럼	deureom
reading	책읽기	chaegilgi
cinema	영화관	yeonghwagwan
play (theater)	연극	yeongeuk
drawing	그림 그리기	geurim geurigi
photography	사진술	sajinsul
hunting	사냥	sanyang
fishing	낚시	naksi
to play (a sport)	하다	hada
to play (strings, percussion/wind, brass)	치다/불다	chida/bulda
to be interested in	관심있다	gwansimitta

FURTHER VOCABULARY

rowing	조정	jojeong
windsurfing	윈드서핑	windeuseoping
diving	잠수, 다이빙	jamsu, daibing
camping	캠핑	kaemping
horseback riding	승마	seungma
horseracing	경마	gyeongma
shooting	사격	sagyeok
fencing	펜싱	pensing

wrestling	레슬링	reseulling
weightlifting	역도	yeokdo
fan	팬	paen
member	회원	hoewon
chess	체스	cheseu
board game	보드 게임	bodeu geim
model	모델	model
to train, to practice	연습하다	yeonseuphada
to go for a walk	산책하다	sanchaekhada
to run, to jog	달리다	dallida
to stretch	뻗치다	ppeochida
to knit	뜨다	tteuda
to cook	음식하다	eumsikhada
to build	짓다	jitta

 USEFUL PHRASES

What do you like to do in your free time?	여가 시간에 뭐하세요?
What's your favorite hobby?	제일 좋아하는 취미가 뭐예요?
What soccer team do you follow?	어느 축구 팀을 지지하세요?
I play the guitar and the piano.	저는 기타와 피아노를 쳐요.
I'm not interested in sports.	저는 운동에 관심이 없어요.
I prefer reading.	책읽기를 선호해요.
I am a member of the club.	클럽 회원이에요.

TOPIC 10
EXERCISES

I. Choose a word from the list below to describe each of the hobbies.

1 _____

2 _____

3 _____

4 _____

5 _____

6 _____

잠수	책읽기	낚시
음악	농구	펜싱

2. How many of the words from the list can you find?

하	모	델	서	이	하	김	이	땅
연	임	계	거	여	을	펜	싱	름
극	신	에	영	화	관	늘	하	옵
에	히	받	이	룩	스	키	루	피
아	다	일	에	루	식	니	옵	아
그	어	선	수	지	뜻	이	에	노
림	것	지	고	늘	시	으	양	이
그	를	운	동	우	달	도	하	리
리	그	할	진	시	리	어	서	주
기	요	나	의	고	기	들	노	래

sports

running

piano

player

song

drawing

cinema

model

play
(theater)

fencing

skiing

3. Arrange the activities below according to where they are normally carried out.

in water	outdoors (on land)	indoors	in a studio

경마 영화보기 다이빙 노래

조정 캠핑 보드 게임 수영

사진술 윈드서핑 배구 체스

농구 역도 낚시 승마

4. Write a paragraph about your hobbies. Use the tables below to help you make sentences.

I	activity	like/prefer	because	description
나는 (I)	축구를 (soccer)	좋아한다 (like)	왜냐하면 (because)	재밌으니까 (it's interesting)
	수영을 (swimming)	선호한다 (prefer)		신나니까 (it's exciting)
	보드게임에 (board games)	관심이 있다 (am interested in)		쉬우니까 (it's easy)
	(etc. see vocabulary list)			몸에 좋으니까 (it's good for the health)

I	at/in	with	verb
저는 (I)	집에서 (at home)	친구랑 (with friends)	놀아요 (play [sports])
	클럽에서 (in the club)	동료들이랑 (with colleagues)	춤춰요 (dance)
	공원에서 (in the park)	식구들이랑 (with members of my family)	연습해요 (practice)

 REMEMBER

In spoken Korean the degree of respect is shown not only by the verb ending but also by the noun or pronoun chosen. The choice indicates the relationship between the speaker and the listener. 저 jeo is a polite way of talking about yourself, but when speaking to a friend or a younger person there is no need to use 저 jeo. You can use the alternative pronoun 나 na instead.

Media

CORE VOCABULARY

media	대중매체	daejungmaechae
communication	통신	tongsin
technology	기술	gisul
broadcast, broadcasting	방송	bangsong
television	텔레비전	telebijeon
radio	라디오	ladio
sound	음향	eumhyang
tape	테이프	teipeu
disc	디스크	diseukeu
recorder	녹음기	nogeumgi
press	출판물	chulpanmul
news	뉴스	nyuseu
newspaper	신문	sinmun
magazine	잡지	jabji
article	논설	nonseol
computer	컴퓨터	keompyuteo
keyboard	키보드	kibodeu
screen	스크린	seukeurin
printer	프린터	peurinteo
scanner	스캐너	seukeneo
file	파일	pail

Internet	인터넷	inteonet
website	웹사이트	websaiteu
channel	채널	chaeneol
telephone	전화기	jeonhwagi
cell phone, mobile phone	휴대폰	hyudaepon
advertisement	광고	gwang-go
program	프로그램	peurogeuraem
journalist	기자	gija
editor	편집자	pyeonjibja
director	감독	gamdok
producer	프로듀서	peurodyuseo
correspondent	통신	tongsin
photographer	사진사	sajinsa
broadcaster, announcer	아나운서	anaunseo
to watch	보다	boda
to listen	듣다	deutta
to record	녹음하다	nogeumhada
to print	복사하다	boksahada
to publish	출판하다	chulpanhada

FURTHER VOCABULARY

press conference	기자 회견	gija hoegyeon
editor-in-chief	편집장	pyeonjibjang
newscast, bulletin	뉴스방송	nyuseu bangsong
transmission	전송	jeongsong
report	리포트	ripoteu
remote control	리모콘	rimokon
soap opera	연속극	yeongsokkeuk
episode	에피소드	eopisodeu

satellite channel	위성 채널	wiseong chaeneol
machine	기계	gigye
worldwide web	월드 와이드 웹	woldeu waideu wep
programmer	프로그래머	peurogeuraemeo
download	다운로드	daunlodeu
log-in name	로그인 이름	logeuin ireum
password	암호	amho
to produce	만들다	mandeulda
to show, run *(program, film)*	상영하다	sangyeonghada
to save, to memorize	저장하다	jeojanghada
to download	다운로드하다	daunlodeu hada

USEFUL PHRASES

Dear viewers, it's time for today's news headlines.	시청자 여러분, 안녕하십니까? 오늘의 주요뉴습니다.
Dear listeners, thank you for listening and goodbye.	청취자 여러분, 오늘도 청취해 주셔서 감사합니다. 안녕히 계십시오.
Generally, I prefer the Internet to newspapers.	저는 보통 신문보다 인터넷을 선호합니다.
This show is very interesting/boring.	이 프로 아주 재미있어요/지루해요.
I like watching Korean films.	한국영화 보는 걸 좋아해요.

EXERCISES

I. Choose a word from the list below to describe each of the pictures.

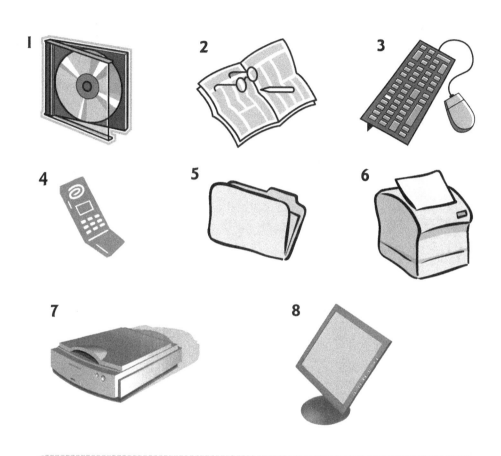

키보드	휴대폰
파일	스캐너
스크린	신문
디스크	프린터

2. Fill in the gaps in the sentences below using the words in the box.

1 나는 한국 영화 _____ 좋아합니다. 하지만 광고는 싫어합니다.

2 요즘엔 인터넷에서 모든 _____를 볼 수 있습니다.

3 하지만 우리 할머니는 아직도 라디오 _____ 좋아합니다.

4 편집자가 이 잡지 _____을 씁니다.

5 이 사설들은 인터넷 _____ 에서도 볼 수 있습니다.

> 웹사이트   듣는 것을   보는 걸   뉴스   사설

 REMEMBER

In written Korean, as used in formal documents, articles, academic papers, and so on, there are polite and plain forms. The polite ending is 습니다 or ㅂ니다, whereas the plain ending is 는다 or ㄴ다.

Polite ending

씁니다 sseubnida *(I) write*

좋아합니다 joh-ahabnida *(I) like*

Plain ending

쓴다 sseunda *(I) write*

좋아한다 joh-ahanda *(I) like*

3. Write six to eight sentences about your preferences when it comes to how you use the media. Use the table below to help you.

I	how often	purpose	media	verb
나는 (I)	항상 (always)	국제 뉴스를 보기위해 (to see the international news)	텔레비전을 (television)	본다 (watch)
	보통 (ususally)	지방 뉴스를 보기 위해 (to see the local news)	라디오를 (radio)	듣는다 (listen)
	가끔 (occasionally)	영화를 보기 위해 (to see movies)	신문을 (newspaper)	읽는다 (read)
	자주 (often)	날씨를 보기 위해 (to see the weather)	인터넷을 (Internet)	뒤진다 (surf)
		연예프로를 보기 위해 (for entertainment)	휴대폰을 (cell phone)	사용한다 (use)

_____

_____

_____

_____

_____

_____

Weather and environment

 ## CORE VOCABULARY

weather	날씨	nalssi
environment	환경	hwangyeong
nature	자연	jayeon
atmosphere, weather	대기	daegi
climate	기후	gihu
season	계절	gyejeol
spring	봄	bom
summer	여름	yeoreum
autumn	가을	gaeul
winter	겨울	gyeoeul
heat	열	yeol
hot	덥다	deobda
clear, fine	맑다	maktta
temperature	온도, 기온	ondo, gion
cold (*noun*)	추위	chuwi
cold (*adjective*)	춥다	chubda
warm	따뜻하다	ttatteuthada
moderate, temperate	적당하다	jeokdanghada
humidity	습도	seubdo
cloud	구름	gureum
rain	비	bi

snow	눈	nun
snowy	눈이 내리다	nuni naerida
sunny	화창하다	hwachanghada
cloudy	구름이 끼다	gureumi kkida
rainy	비가 내리다	biga naerida
sky	하늘	haneul
earth, land	땅	ttang
sun	해, 태양	hae, taeyang
moon	달	dal
water	물	mul
air	공기	gong-gi
earth, dust	흙	heuk
fire	불	bul
wind	바람	baram
storm	폭풍	pokpung
pollution	공해	gonghae
cause, reason	이유	iyu
to cause	초래하다	choraehada
to protect	보호하다	bohohada

FURTHER VOCABULARY

fog	안개	angae
flood	홍수	hongsu
earthquake	지진	jijin
tornado	토네이도	toneido
protection	방어	bango
planet	행성	haengseong
the globe, the earth	지구	jigu
natural	자연의	jayeongui

organic	유기의	yugiui
harm	해	hae
poisonous	독성분의	dokseongbunui
lightning	번개	beongae
sandstorm	모래폭풍	moraepokpung
snowstorm	폭설	pokseol
heat wave	폭서	pokseo
shade	그늘	geuneul
wet	젖다	jeotta
dry	건조하다	geonjohada
drought	가뭄	gamum
to pollute	오염되다	oyeomdoeda
to blow *(the wind)*	불다	bulda

 # USEFUL PHRASES

How's the weather today?	오늘 날씨 어때요?
The weather is cold/hot/sunny.	날씨가 추워요/더워요/화창해요.
Snow is falling.	눈이 내려요
The wind is blowing.	바람이 불어요.
The temperature is high/low.	온도가 높아요/낮아요.
The Earth's temperature has risen greatly in recent years.	최근 지구의 온도가 급격히 상승했다.
Modern factories are one of the causes of pollution.	현대의 공장들이 오염을 초래한다.

TOPIC 12
EXERCISES

1. Complete the crossword using the clues provided.

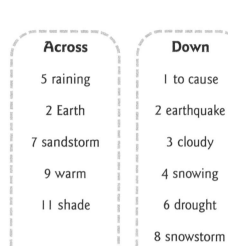

Across

5 raining

2 Earth

7 sandstorm

9 warm

11 shade

Down

1 to cause

2 earthquake

3 cloudy

4 snowing

6 drought

8 snowstorm

10 sky

2. Put the words in order, from the hottest to the coldest.

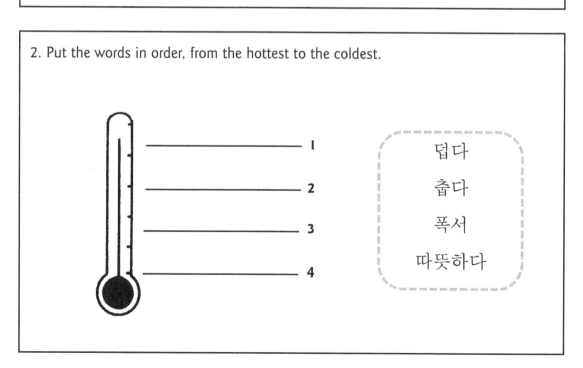

덥다

춥다

폭서

따뜻하다

3. Describe the weather in each picture. The words you need are all in the main vocabulary lists.

1 _____ 내려요.

2 날씨가 _____ .

3 _____ 꼈어요.

4 _____ 내려요.

4. Make a weather diary for the week, using the table below to help you.

day of the week	time of day	weather	description	temperature/ humidity	level
일요일 (Sunday)	아침에 (in the morning)	날씨가... (the weather is...)	화창하고 (sunny)	기온이... (and the temperature is...)	높습니다 (high)
월요일 (Monday)	오후에 (in the afternoon)		좋고 (fine)		적당합니다 (moderate)
화요일 (Tuesday)	저녁에 (in the evening)		비가 내리고 (rainy)	습도가... (and the humidity is...)	낮습니다 (low)
수요일 (Wednesday)	밤에 (at night)		눈이 내리고 (snowy)		
목요일 (Thursday)			덥고 (hot)		
금요일 (Friday)			춥고 (cold)		
토요일 (Saturday)			etc.		

 REMEMBER

Conjunctions (joining words) can be used in Korean between sentences or within a sentence. If used within a sentence, only the last syllable or two of the conjunction are used. The most common conjunctions are 그리고 (고) geurigo (go) meaning *and*, 그렇지만 (지만) geurechiman (jiman) meaning *but* and 그래서 (서) geuraeseo (seo) meaning *so*.

비가 내립니다. 그리고 기온이 낮습니다. *It's raining, And the temperature is low.*
or 비가 내리고 기온이 낮습니다. *It's raining, and the temperature is low.*
눈이 내립니다. 그렇지만 따뜻합니다. *It's snowing, But it's warm.*
or 눈이 내리지만 따뜻합니다. *It's snowing, but it's warm.*

Local Area

CORE VOCABULARY

region	지역	jiyeok
place	장소	jangso
city	도시	dosi
countryside	시골	sigol
village	마을	maeul
district, quarter	구	gu
street, road, way	길	gil
traffic	교통	gyotong
congestion	체증	chejeung
downtown	시내	sinae
complex *(offices, apartments, etc.)*	단지	danji
school	학교	hakgyo
hotel	호텔	hotel
restaurant	식당	sikdang
pharmacy	약국	yakguk
bank	은행	eunhaeng
park	공원	gongwon
police station	경찰서	gyeongchalseo
gas station	주유소	juyuso
palace	궁전	gungjeon

temple	신전, 절	sinjeon, jeol
church	교회	gyohoe
library	도서관	doseogwan
zoo	동물원	dongmulwon
pagoda	탑	tap
museum	박물관	bangmulgwan
post office	우체국	ucheguk
movie theater	영화관	yeonghwagwan
theater	극장	geukjang
bridge	다리	dari
farm	농장	nongjang
mountain	산	san
beach	해변	haebyeon
river	강	gang
north	북쪽	bukjjok
west	서쪽	seojjok
south	남쪽	namjjok
east	동쪽	dongjjok
to park *(a vehicle)*	주차하다	juchahada
to get lost	길을 잃다	gireul iltta

FURTHER VOCABULARY

townhall	도청, 시청	docheong, sicheong
club	클럽	keulleop
café	카페	kape
bookstore	서점	seojeom
synagogue	유대교 회당	yudaegyo hoedang
mosque	회교 사원	hoegyo sawon
building	빌딩	bilding

skyscraper	고층 건물	gocheung geonmul
suburb	교외	gyo-oe
sports center	스포츠 센터	seupocheu senteo
garage	차고	chago
corner	모퉁이	motungi
forest	삼림	samlim
hill	언덕	eondeok
to roam around	배회하다	baehoehada
to establish, to found	설립하다	seollibhada

 # USEFUL PHRASES

Excuse me, where's the police station?	실례합니다만, 경찰서가 어디예요?
Is this the way to the Old City?	이 길이 구시가지로 가는 길인가요?
Go straight ahead.	직진하세요.
Take the first street on the right/left.	첫번째 골목에서 오른쪽으로/왼쪽으로 가세요.
Is there a bank near here?	가까운 곳에 은행이 있나요?
The park is located in front of the Deoksu Palace.	공원은 덕수궁 앞에 위치해 있어요.

EXERCISES

I. Match the words below with the numbered features in the town.

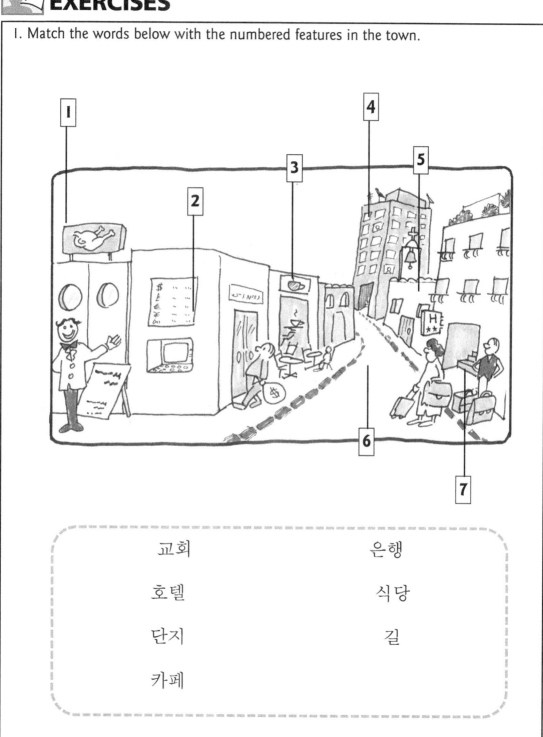

교회   은행

호텔   식당

단지   길

카페

2. How many of the words can you find in the word search?

낙	지	내	시	골	람	어	교	기	도
단	엽	가	바	한	은	은	통	슬	시
지	마	어	언	딜	장	소	에	서	아
나	이	람	덕	잎	떨	두	며	쪽	는
둥	마	을	음	비	조	살	입	게	피
고	에	시	도	길	잃	교	통	체	증
게	글	짝	바	려	돌	가	약	라	러
지	역	달	도	고	층	건	물	아	무

region   congestion   hill   place

traffic   road   west   complex

countryside   village   city   skyscraper

 REMEMBER

에 e, 에서 eseo and 으로 euro are particles commonly used to express the equivalent of *in, at, on, to* or *from*. You will need try to remember the correct usage of each.

에 e: 은행에 가요. *I'm going to the bank.*

           서울에 살아요. *I live in Seoul.*

           월요일에 만나요. *I'll meet you on Monday.*

에서 eseo: 공원에서 놀아요. *I play in the park.*

           서울에서 왔어요. *I'm from Seoul.*

으로 euro: 왼쪽으로 가세요. *Go (to) the left.*

3. Here is a description of the area where someone lives:

저는 저는 공주라고 불리는 도시에 살아요. 서부지방에
위치해 있어요.

공주에는 대학교 두 개와 새로지은 큰 도서관이 있어요.
영화관이 많이 있지만 극장은 없어요.

교외에는 강을 낀 농장이 있고 절도 볼 수 있어요.

Now write a similar paragraph about where you live.
Use the following phrases to help you:

- **I live in a town/village called...**   저는 ...라고 불리는 도시/마을에 살아요.

- **It is situated in...**   ...에 위치해 있어요.

- **There is/are...,**   ...이 있어요,

- **but there is no/are no...**   ...있지만 ...은 없어요.

- **... can be found.**   ...도 볼 수 있어요.

_____

_____

_____

_____

_____

Travel and tourism

CORE VOCABULARY

travel, journey, trip	여행	yeohaeng
tourism	관광	gwangwang
visit	방문하다	bangmunhada
country	나라	nara
traveler	여행객	yeohaeng-gaek
car	자동차	jadongcha
taxi	택시	taeksi
bicycle	자전거	jajeongeo
train	기차	gicha
plane	비행기	bihaeng-gi
boat	보트	boteu
ship	배	bae
bus	버스	beoseu
airport	공항	gonghang
bus stop	버스 정류장	beoseu jeongnyujang
station	역	yeok
port, harbor	항구	hang-gu
passport	여권	yeogwon
visa	비자	bija
ticket	표	pyo
one-way	편도	pyeondo

roundtrip (ticket)	왕복표	wangbokpyo
sea	바다	bada
seaside	바닷가	badatga
baggage	짐	jim
camera	카메라	kamera
postcard	엽서	yeobseo
fast	빠르다	ppareuda
slow	느리다	neurida
straight on	바로	baro
abroad	해외	haeoe
before	전	jeon
after	후	hu
to go	가다	gada
to walk	걷다	geotta
to return	돌아오다	doraoda
to travel	여행가다	yeohaeng-gada
to ride, to catch, to board	타다	tada
to spend (time)	쓰다	sseuda
to arrive	도착하다	dochakhada

FURTHER VOCABULARY

public transportation	대중 교통	daejung gyotong
means of transportation	교통 수단	gyotong sudan
seat	자리	jari
crossroad	교차로	gyocharo
traffic lights	신호등	sinhodeung
railway	철도	cheoldo
campsite	야영지	yayeongji
tunnel	터널	teoneol

subway	지하철	jihacheol
coach	고속버스	gosokbeoseu
on time	정시	jeongsi
youth hostel	유스호스텔	yuseu hoseutel
to take off	이륙하다	iryukhada
to land	착륙하다	changnyukhada
to cross	건너다	geonneoda
to hurry	서두르다	seodureuda
to receive	받다	batta
to welcome	환영하다	hwanyeonghada

 # USEFUL PHRASES

Have a nice stay!	좋은 시간 되세요.
Have a nice trip!	좋은 여행 되세요.
We spent six days in Busan.	부산에서 육일 지냈어요.
We reserved a room overlooking the sea.	바다가 보이는 방을 예약했어요.
We want to reserve seats on the train.	기차표를 예약하고 싶은데요.
Is there air conditioning?	에어콘 있나요?

EXERCISES

I. Find words in the vocabulary list to describe the pictures below.

1 _____   2 _____

3 _____   4 _____

5 _____   6 _____

REMEMBER

When talking about means of transportation, we use the preposition 로 ro *by*.

버스로 바닷가에 가요. *(I) go to the beach by bus.*

기차로 경주에 가요. *(I) go to Gyeongju by train.*

2. Complete the crossword using the clues provided.

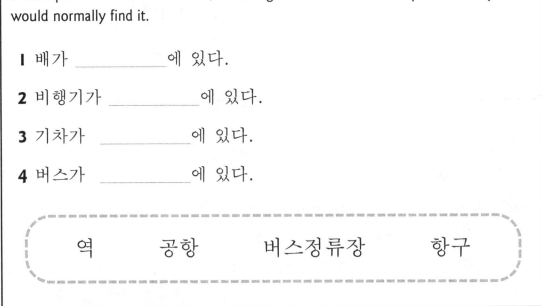

Across

3 tourist

4 subway

5 sea

7 youth hostel

Down

1 plane

2 to welcome

3 passport

6 traffic lights

3. Complete the sentences below, matching each vehicle with the place where you would normally find it.

1 배가 _____에 있다.

2 비행기가 _____에 있다.

3 기차가 _____에 있다.

4 버스가 _____에 있다.

역   공항   버스정류장   항구

4. You are planning a trip involving several stops, and using different modes of transportation. Write a paragraph about the trip with the help of the table below.

sequence	from	to	transportation	to travel
먼저 (first)			버스로 (by bus)	여행가요. (I travel)
그리고 (then)			기차로 (by train)	가요. (I go)
그리고 나서 (after that)	...에서 (from...)	...까지 (to...)	비행기로 (by plane)	
마지막으로 (finally)			배로 (by ship)	
			차로 (by car)	
			자전거로 (by bicycle)	

_____

_____

_____

_____

_____

TOPIC 15

Education

CORE VOCABULARY

student, pupil	학생	haksaeng
teacher	교사, 선생님	gyosa, seonsaengnim
professor	교수	gyosu
elementary school	초등학교	chodeunghakgyo
middle school	중학교	junghakgyo
high school	고등학교	godeunghakgyo
faculty	학부	hakbu
university, college	대학교	daehakgyo
academy	학원	hakwon
class, classroom	교실	gyosil
semester, term	학기	hakgi
lesson	수업	sueop
homework	숙제	sukje
book	책	chaek
exercise book	연습장	yeonseubjang
pen	펜	pen
pencil	연필	yeonpil
eraser	지우개	jiugae
pencil sharpener	연필깎기	yeonpilkkakki
ruler	자	ja
notebook	공책	gongchaek

dictionary	사전	sajeon
letter *(of the alphabet)*	문자	munja
number	번호	beonho
question	질문	jilmun
answer	답	dap
exam	시험	siheom
mathematics	수학	suhak
literature	문학	munhak
English language	영어	yeongeo
Korean language	한국어	hangugeo
history	역사	yeoksa
geography	지리	jiri
science	과학	gwahak
biology	생물학	saengmulhak
chemistry	화학	hwahak
physics	물리학	mullihak
to study	공부하다	gongbuhada
to teach	가르치다	gareuchida
to learn	배우다	baeuda

FURTHER VOCABULARY

headteacher, principal	교장선생님	gyojang-seonsaengnim
school administration	학교 행정	hakgyo haengjeong
registration	등록	deungnok
admissions office	입학관리처	ibhak-gwallicheo
period, lesson	마침표	machimpyo
timetable	시간표	siganpyo
page	쪽	jjok
ink	잉크	ingkeu

scholarship	장학금	janghakgeum
board	위원회	wiwonhoe
chalk	분필	bunpil
school uniform	교복	gyobok
private school	사립학교	saribhakgyo
nursery	유치원	yuchiwon
psychology	심리학	simnihak
sociology	사회학	sahoehak
education	교육학	gyoyukhak
economics	경제학	gyeongjehak
to revise	복습하다	bokseubhada
to ask	묻다	mutta
to answer	대답하다	daedabhada
to enroll	등록하다	deungnokhada
to look for, to search	찾다	chatta
to memorize	외우다	oeuda

USEFUL PHRASES

Raise your hand.	손을 드세요.
Take out your pen.	볼펜을 꺼내세요.
Open your books.	책을 펴세요.
Do you have any questions?	질문 있어요?

(See also list of instructions on page 105.)

EXERCISES

I. Choose a word from the vocabulary list to describe each of the pictures.

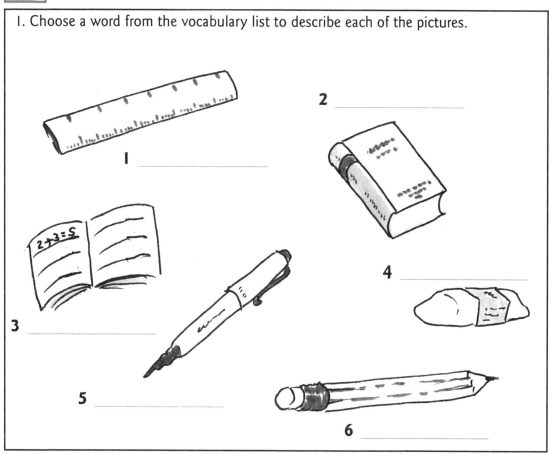

1 _____

2 _____

3 _____

4 _____

5 _____

6 _____

REMEMBER

In Korean the present tense endings (요, 세요) can also be used with a future meaning. However, when you want to emphsise the intention, use the future tense ending (ㄹ거예요).

내년에 한국에 가요. *I'll go to Korea next year.*

내일 친구 만나세요? *Will you meet your friend tomorrow?*

내년에 한국에 갈거예요. *I'll go to Korea next year,*

내일 친구 만날거예요? *Will you meet your friend tomorrow?*

2. Write the English translation next to the Korean words.

1 질문 _____   **5** 자 _____

2 교실 _____   **6** 학교 _____

3 대학교 _____   **7** 공책 _____

4 번호 _____   **8** 책 _____

3. Fill in the blanks with the appropriate verb or phrase from the box below.

1 저는 학생이에요. 그리고 대학교에서 영문학을 _____.

2 저저는 프랑스에 여행가서 불어를 _____.

3 저는 교육학 교수예요. 그리고 심리학을 _____.

4 저는 오월에 있을 시험을 위해 _____.

5 책 65쪽을 _____.

6 우리 아버지는 어렸을 때 많은 시를 _____.

7 학생들이 인터넷에서 질문의 답을 _____.

8 학교에서 불어도 _____?

가르쳐요	배울거예요	공부하세요
외웠어요	복습해요	공부해요
펴세요	찾고 있어요	

4. Look at JinHi's timetable for Monday and Tuesday. Make sentences about what he studies in every class, as in the example. (*Note:* 오전 ojeon = am; 오후 ohu = pm)

	오전8.00–9.30	오전9.30–11.15	오전11.30–오후1.00	오후2.00–3.30
월요일 Monday	역사 History	화학 Chemistry	한국어 Korean	체육 P.E.
화요일 Tuesday	영어 English	지리 Geography	생물학 Biology	물리학 Physics

진희는 월요일에 여덟시부터 아홉시 반까지 역사를 공부합니다.

JinHi studies History on Monday from 8 o'clock until half past nine.

_____

_____

_____

_____

_____

_____

TOPIC 16
Work

CORE VOCABULARY

work	일	il
job, position	직업	jigeop
profession	전문 직업	jeonmun jigeop
company	회사	hoesa
branch	지사	jisa
office	사무실	samusil
experience	경험	gyeongheom
trade	무역	muyeok
employer, boss	고용주	goyongju
manager, director	관리자	gwallija
worker, employee	직원	jigwon
businessman/businesswoman	사업가	saeobga
secretary	비서	biseo
employee	근로자	geulloja
civil servant	공무원	gongmuwon
expert	전문가	jeonmunga
researcher	연구원	yeonguwon
doctor	의사	uisa
trader	무역업자	muyeogeobja
lawyer	변호사	byeonhosa
judge	판사	pansa

English	Korean	Romanization
engineer	엔지니어	enjinieo
mechanic	기계공	gigyegong
pilot	조종사	jojongsa
driver	운전사	unjeonsa
electrician	전기공	jeongigong
plumber	배관공	baegwangong
cook	요리사	yorisa
scientist	과학자	gwahakja
barber	이발사	ibalsa
florist	꽃장수	kkotjangsu
farmer	농부	nongbu
artist	예술가	yesulga
unemployment	실업	sireop
unemployed	실업자	sireobja
retirement	퇴직	toejik
retired	퇴직하다	toejikhada
salary	월급	wolgeup
to work	일하다	ilhada
to employ	고용하다	goyonghada

FURTHER VOCABULARY

English	Korean	Romanization
ambitious	야망	yamang
gifted	재능있다	jaeneungitta
project	프로젝트	peurojekteu
plan	계획	gyehoek
future	장래	jangnae
organization	기관	gigwan
commodity	생필품	saengpilpum
job vacancy	공석	gongseok

office, factory	관공서	gwangongseo
consultant	고문	gomun
agent, representative	대리인	daeriin
accountant	회계사	hoegyesa
translator	번역자	beonyeokja
interpreter	통역	tongyeok
pension	연금	yeongeum
part-time	아르바이트	areubaiteu
full-time	전임	jeonim
exploitation	개척	gaecheok
insurance	보험	boheom
to succeed	성공하다	seong-gonghada
to fail	실패하다	silpaehada
to fire	해고되다	haegodoeda
to earn	벌다	beolda
to make, to manufacture	만들다	mandeulda
to pay	지불하다	jibulhada
to run, to manage	경영하다	gyeongyeonghada

USEFUL PHRASES

What does your father/mother do?	어머니/아버지는 뭐 하세요?
Do you have a plan for the future?	장래 계획이 있어요?
I want to be/become an engineer.	엔지니어가 되고 싶어요.
I want to work in a big company.	큰 회사에서 일하고 싶어요.
Currently, I am looking for work.	현재 일을 찾고 있어요.
I work part time every Sunday.	매주 일요일마다 아르바이트를 해요.

EXERCISES

I. Choose a word from the vocabulary list to describe each of the professions.

1 _____

2 _____

3 _____

4 _____

5 _____

6 _____

7 _____

8 _____

2. Circle the odd-one-out in each set of words.

1 일	예술가	전문직업	직업
2 사무실	회사	기관	실업
3 배관공	전기공	장래	엔지니어
4 메니저	상사	생필품	직원
5 판사	연금	월급	보험

3. Fill in the blanks with the appropriate verb from the box below.

저는 대학에서 생물학을 _____. 매주 토요일과

일요일마다 수퍼마켓에서 _____. 토요일에 6시간

_____ 일요일에 4시간 _____. 제 장래

희망은 _____. 큰 회사에서 일하고 _____.

일하고	공부해요
싶어요	일해요
아르바이트 해요	과학자예요

4. Talk about your profession and/or the professions of your family and friends, with the help of the table below.

who	description	place	profession	verb
저는 *(I)*	큰 *(big)*	회사에서 *(company)*	연구원으로 *(a researcher)*	일하고 있어요. *(work)*
제 오빠는 *(my brother)*	작은 *(small)*	은행에서 *(bank)*	매니저로 *(a manager)*	
제 여동생은 *(my sister)*	새로운 *(new)*	기관에서 *(organization)*	교사로 *(a teacher)*	
제 아버지는 *(my father)*	오랜 *(old)*	식당에서 *(restaurant)*	*etc.*	
제 어머니는 *(my mother)*	외국 *(foreign)*	*etc.*		
제 친구는 *(my friend)*	유명한 *(famous)*			

저는 유명한 식당에서 요리사로 일하고 있어요.
I work in a famous restaurant as a chef.

 REMEMBER

The verb ending –고 있어요 -go isseoyo denotes the present continuous tense.

직장을 찾고 있어요. *I'm looking for a job.*

텔레비전을 보고 있어요. *I'm watching TV.*

Examination tips and instructions in Korean

PREPARING FOR EXAMINATIONS

Once you have worked your way through this book, you will have the solid foundation in Korean vocabulary that you need to tackle examinations. Each examination has its own demands, so it is best to know what they are and tailor your preparation according to them.

1   Obtain examples of past papers and *go through them systematically*. Make a note of words that occur frequently. It may be that you already know most of the words, but watch out for new ones and make sure you learn them. Many examinations reuse a lot of vocabulary, so being familiar with the content of past papers is a sound strategy.

2   There are some things you might need to learn in addition to what you find in this book.
    • If you are at college or university, it is likely that there are particular texts that you need to be familiar with.
    • If you are preparing for a professional qualification in a particular field, it is important to know the technical vocabulary associated with it.

3   It is essential to know how the exam works. Find out about the grading scheme, so you have a clear idea of what you need to do for each question and how much time you are going to spend on it. (And make sure the information you have about the examination is up to date.)

4   If the instructions and questions are going to be in Korean, you will need to know what form they normally take. (You do not want to lose points because you did not understand what you had to do.) Opposite are some key Korean instructions often found in examinations.

INSTRUCTIONS IN KOREAN

Read the following text.	아래 문장을 읽으세요.
Look at the picture in front of you.	앞에 있는 그림을 보세요.
Listen to the announcement/ news report/dialog.	다음의 공지사항/뉴스 보도/대화를 잘 들으세요.
Answer the following questions.	다음의 질문에 답하세요.
Write the appropriate word/a summary/ a commentary/an analysis.	적당한 단어/요약/논평/ 비평을 쓰세요.
Put a [✔] in front of the correct sentence.	맞는 문장에 표[✔]하세요.
Fill in the blank with the appropriate word.	적당한 단어를 빈 칸에 넣으세요.
Complete the following sentences.	문장을 완성하세요.
Say.../ Describe...	... 말하세요. /... 설명하세요.
Summarize.../ Define...	... 요약하세요. / ...정의하세요.
Write a letter/a postcard.	편지/엽서를 쓰세요.
Explain the meaning of the following phrases/words.	아래 구절/단어를 설명하세요.
Briefly mention the reasons.	이유를 설명하세요.
Answer the letter.	편지에 답장하세요.
Use the following words/phrases.	다음의 단어/구절을 사용하세요.
Use your own words as much as possible.	최대한 본인의 말을 사용하세요.
...as shown in the example.	예문에서 보여준 바와 같이.

Answers to exercises

This section gives model answers for the exercises. Note that there are no definitive answers to the final freestyle exercises and compositions in each topic.
Try to check your answers with a Korean-speaking friend or teacher.

TOPIC 1 BASIC EXPRESSIONS

Exercise 1

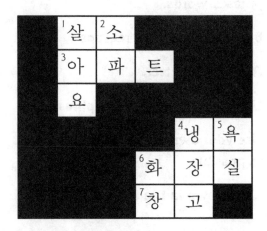

Exercise 2
See list page 9 for answers.

Exercise 3

1 고양이가 차 위에 있어요.

2 고양이가 차 안에 있어요.

3 고양이가 차 아래에 있어요.

4 고양이가 차 옆에 있어요.

Exercise 4

안녕하세요, 민준씨.

생일 축하해요!

어떻게 지내셨어요?
저는 잘 지내요.

좋은 시간 되세요.

TOPIC 2 HOUSE AND HOME

Exercise 1

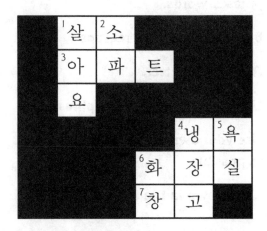

Exercise 2

Exercise 3

a 집이 커요.

b 빌라가 낡았어요.

c 승강기가 복잡해요.

d 가구가 달린 아파트예요.

e 방이 편안해요.

Exercise 4

TOPIC 3 FAMILY AND FRIENDS

Exercise 1

가	남	해	주	요	제	사	미
족	람	총	각	남	아	친	영
진	가	마	소	낭	포	구	배
유	진	어	가	고	남	이	새
로	찬	린	부	머	자	나	모
종	과	이	거	국	애	일	행
본	라	음	모	비	잔	우	마
세	타	건	어	머	니	수	벼
여	대	남	악	학	이	주	방
남	편	포	소	기	여	자	애

Exercise 2

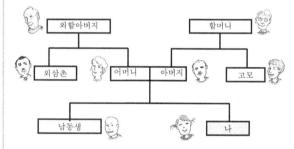

Exercise 3

Top left: 언니 *(older sister to a female)*, 누나 *(older sister to a male)*

Top right: 이모 *(aunt, maternal)*, 고모 *(aunt, paternal)*

Bottom left: 청소년 *(adolescent)*, 청년 *(youth)*, 총각 *(single)*

Bottom right: 어린이 *(child)*, 남자애 *(boy)*, 여자애 *(girl)*

Exercise 4

1 제 친구 남편이 죽었어요. 제 친구는 과부예요.

2 우리 여동생이 9월에 결혼해요. 남편을 대학교에서 만났어요.

3 우리 어머니는 언니가 둘, 동생이 하나예요. 그래서 저는 이모가 세 명이에요.

4 저는 아이가 넷이에요. 딸 셋 그리고 아들 하나예요.

TOPIC 4 CHARACTER AND FEELINGS

Exercise 1

1 행복해요	2 슬퍼요
3 화났어요	4 튼튼해요
5 웃겨요	6 지루해요

Exercise 2

1 슬퍼요	2 약해요
3 조용해요	4 멍청해요
5 관대해요	

Exercise 3

(Your answers may vary.)

매우 긍정적	긍정적	부정적	매우 부정적
즐거워요	좋아요	지루해요	괴로워요
행복해요	활동적이에요	약해요	게을러요
진실해요	웃겨요	두려워요	끔찍해요
신실해요	참아요	시끄러워요	무례해요
관대해요	조용해요	실망했어요	
근면해요	행실이 좋아요	외로워요	
유쾌해요	튼튼해요	이기적이에요	
지혜로워요	이치에 맞아요	화났어요	
용감해요		인색해요	

TOPIC 5 SHOPPING

Exercise 1

1 닫아요 2 열어요   3 싸다   4 비싸다
5 생선가게   6 병   7 재단사   8 가방

Exercise 2

A5   B6   C3   D1   E4   F2

Exercise 3

1 화폐 2 병   3 점원   4 백화점

TOPIC 6 CLOTHES AND COLORS

Exercise 1

1 신발   2 드레스   3 치마
4 목돌이   5 양말   6 드레싱 가운
7 모자   8 혁대

Exercise 2

1 목걸이   2 바지   3 사이즈   4 신발

Exercise 3

바지 2	블라우스 1	장갑 4	양말 5
목걸이 3	반지 3	치마 2	청바지 2
자켓 1	혁대 4	신발 5	샌달 5
목돌이 4	모자 4	스웨터 1	귀걸이 3

TOPIC 7 FOOD AND DRINK

Exercise 1

1 주스   2 차   3 커피
4 생선   5 빵   6 당근
7 냄비   8 닭고기

Exercise 2

fruit/과일	drinks/음료수
오렌지	우유
사과	사과 주스
포도	물
체리	코카콜라
바나나	오렌지 주스
딸기	

vegetables/채소
버섯
양파
오이
올리브
당근

Exercise 3

1 닭고기   2 버터   3 메뉴   4 후식

TOPIC 8 THE BODY

Exercise 1

가	봉	엄	지	손	가	락
등	주	솜	재	민	신	바
나	책	입	술	기	초	염
눈	치	매	질	손	춘	호
다	재	영	람	가	공	즈
옴	다	새	여	락	토	마
비	리	밀	데	너	직	어
펴	자	아	듬	진	려	호
자	다	얼	굴	반	사	배
머	리	장	및	앵	주	차

Exercise 2

손으로 만져요
귀로 들어요
코로 냄새맡아요
눈으로 봐요
혀로 맛봐요

Exercise 3

1 머리   2 눈   3 코   4 귀   5 입   6 어깨
7 가슴   8 팔   9 배   10 손가락   11 손
12 다리   13 무릎   14 발   15 발가락

TOPIC 9 HEALTH

Exercise 1

통	고	구	살	열	즈	수	땀	얠	두	츳	미
맥	쎄	ㄷ	먼	너	주	ㅁ	기	빼	지	신	어
딴	웅	양	건	오	치	딴	생	땨	멜	썰	뉵
분	간	우	강	체	선	습	유	소	고	뵈	되
뼈	기	나	화	감	제	편	양	뫈	금	소	다
오	결	불	다	퐈	자	양	기	구	고	탕	쁜
쥬	면	노	뉴	포	티	켱	뼈	제	묘	치	지
ㅎ	다	쁘	오	사	을	섬	퐈	제	기	삐	구
뵈	왜	외	가	기	땶	수	그	늚	촉	은	쁜
띤	키	근	껌	쳥	얺	쯧	다	우	뵈	또	땁

Exercise 2

(Your answers may vary.)

Things used in the treatment of illness and injury:
약   알약   체온계   처방전
휠체어   구급차

Types of injury:
일사병   화상   물집   상처   멍

Types of illness:
두통   당뇨   암   독감   수두   홍역
정신병

Exercise 3

1 저는 담배를 많이 피워요. 가끔은 하루에 40 개비를 피워요.

2 사고 이후에 차 안에만 있으면 스트레스로 고통을 받아요.

3 밥을 먹은 후에 민주는 배가 아팠어요.

4 기침과 재채기를 왜 그렇게 하세요? 감기 걸렸어요?

TOPIC 10 HOBBIES

Exercise 1

1 농구
2 낚시
3 잠수
4 펜싱
5 책읽기
6 음악

Exercise 2

하	모	델	서	이	하	김	이	땅
연	임	계	거	여	을	펜	싱	름
극	신	에	영	화	관	늘	하	옵
에	히	받	이	룩	스	키	루	피
아	다	일	에	루	식	니	옵	아
그	어	선	수	지	뜻	이	에	노
림	것	지	고	늘	시	으	양	이
그	를	운	동	우	달	도	하	리
리	그	할	진	시	리	어	서	주
기	요	나	의	고	기	들	노	래

Exercise 3

(Your answers may vary.)

in water:	in a studio:
조정	사진술
윈드서핑	노래
다이빙	
수영	

outdoors:

경마
캠핑
낚시
승마

indoors:

농구
영화보기
역도
배구
보드 게임
체스

TOPIC 11 MEDIA

Exercise 1

1 디스크   2 신문   3 키보드   4 휴대폰
5 파일   6 프린터   7 스캐너   8 스크린

Exercise 2

1 나는 한국 영화 보는 걸 좋아합니다. 하지만 광고는 싫어합니다.

2 요즘엔 인터넷에서 모든 뉴스를 볼 수 있습니다.

3 하지만 우리 할머니는 아직도 라디오 듣는 것을 좋아합니다.

4 편집자가 이 잡지 사설을 씁니다.

5 이 사설들은 인터넷 웹사이트에서도 볼 수 있습니다.

TOPIC 12 WEATHER AND ENVIRONMENT

Exercise 1

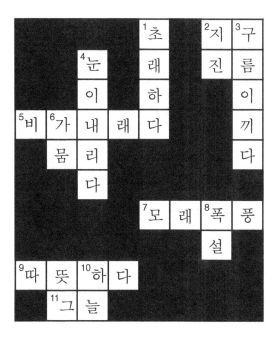

Exercise 2

1 폭서
2 덥다
3 따뜻하다
4 춥다

Exercise 3

1 눈이 내려요.
2 날씨가 화창해요.
3 구름이 꼈어요.
4 비가 내려요.

TOPIC 13 LOCAL AREA

Exercise 1

1 식당	2 은행
3 카페	4 단지
5 교회	6 길
7 호텔	

Exercise 2

지	계	고	어	나	지	단	나
요	글	외	무	의	무	엄	지
멀	쪽	시	을	람	오	가	내
도	부	도	마	달	연	부	시
고	댐	걸	미	요	를	완	글
충	둘	음	조	딸	장	는	람
건	가	교	술	누	수	는	오
물	유	통	업	표	의	옹	교
우	따	체	계	쭝	서	슬	기
무	답	응	피	는	우	시	도

TOPIC 14 TRAVEL AND TOURISM

Exercise 1

1 기차
2 비행기
3 배
4 버스
5 자전거
6 차

Exercise 2

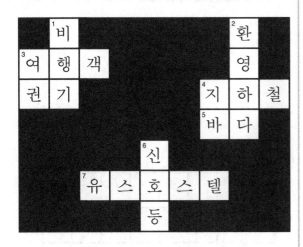

Exercise 3

1 배가 항구에 있다.
2 비행기가 공항에 있다.
3 기차가 역에 있다.
4 버스가 버스정류장에 있다.

TOPIC 15 EDUCATION

Exercise 1

1 자	2 책
3 연습장	4 지우개
5 볼펜	6 연필

Exercise 2

1 question

2 classroom

3 university

4 number

5 ruler

6 school

7 notebook

8 book

Exercise 3

1 저는 학생이에요. 그리고 대학교에서 영문학을 공부해요.
2 저는 프랑스에 여행가서 불어를 배울거예요.
3 저는 교육학 교수예요. 그리고 심리학을 가르쳐요.
4 저는 오월에 있을 시험을 위해 복습해요.
5 책 65쪽을 펴세요.
6 우리 아버지는 어렸을 때 많은 시를 외웠어요.
7 학생들이 인터넷에서 질문의 답을 찾고 있어요.
8 학교에서 불어도 공부하세요?

TOPIC 16 WORK

Exercise 1

1 이발사	2 조종사
3 예술가	4 꽃장수
5 판사	6 전기공
7 요리사	8 기계공

Exercise 2

1 예술가

2 실업

3 장래

4 생필품

5 판사

Exercise 3

저는 대학에서 생물학을 공부해요. 매주 토요일과 일요일마다 수퍼마켓에서 아르바이트 해요. 토요일에 6시간 일하고 일요일에 4시간 일해요. 제 장래 계획은 과학자예요. 큰 회사에서 일하고 싶어요.

hi *(plain)*	excuse me?	which one?	next to
hello *(informal, honorific)*	sorry!/ excuse me!	opposite	inside
hello *(formal, honorific)*	yes	between	outside
bye *(to one leaving/ staying, plain)*	no	toward	I *(plain/polite)*
goodbye *(to one leaving/ staying, honorific)*	what?	around	you *(plain/polite)*
see you again	who?	in	he
welcome	where?	out	she
pleased to meet you	when?	above	it
thank you	how?	on	we
you're welcome	why?	below	they

옆	어떤거?	실례합니다	안녕
안쪽	맞은편	죄송합니다!	안녕하세요?
바깥쪽	사이	네	안녕하십니까?
나/저	향해	아니오	잘 가/ 잘 있어
너/당신	주위	뭐?	안녕히 가세요/ 안녕히 계세요
그	안	누구?	또 만나요
그녀	밖	어디?	환영합니다
그것	위	언제?	만나서 반갑습니다
우리	위	어떻게?	고맙습니다/ 감사합니다
그들	아래	왜?	천만에요

live, reside ②	modern ②	dining room ②	refrigerator ②
house ②	quiet ②	office, study ②	table ②
apartment ②	crowded ②	kitchen ②	chair ②
villa ②	comfortable ②	bathroom ②	door ②
apartment building ②	furnished ②	garden ②	window ②
district, area ②	floor *(level)* ②	carpet ②	bell ②
street ②	lift, elevator ②	curtain ②	air-conditioning ②
small ②	room ②	sofa ②	toilet ②
big, large ②	bedroom ②	bed ②	rent ②
old ②	living room ②	oven ②	to rent ②

냉장고	식당	현대적이에요	살아요
상	공부방	조용해요	집
의자	부엌	복잡해요	아파트
문	욕실	편안해요	빌라
창문	정원	가구가 달렸어요	아파트 단지
종	카페트	층	지역
에어콘	커튼	승강기	거리
화장실	소파	방	작아요
임차	침대	침실	커요
임대	오븐	거실	낡았어요

family ③	daughter ③	grandson ③	single (f) ③
relative ③	wife ③	granddaughter ③	child ③
father ③	husband ③	nephew, niece ③	baby ③
mother ③	boy ③	bride ③	man ③
parents ③	girl ③	bridegroom ③	woman ③
older brother ③ (to a female/to a male)	uncle ③ (paternal/maternal)	married ③	youth ③
younger brother ③	aunt ③ (paternal/maternal)	marriage ③	friend ③
older sister ③ (to a female/to a male)	cousin ③ (paternal/maternal)	divorced ③	was born ③
younger sister ③	grandfather ③ (paternal/maternal)	divorce ③	died ③ (plain/honorific)
son ③	grandmother ③ (paternal/maternal)	single (m) ③	get married (I) ③

처녀	손자	딸	가족
어린이	손녀	아내	친척
아기	조카	남편	아버지
남자	신부	남자애	어머니
여자	신랑	여자애	부모님
청년	결혼했어요	삼촌/외삼촌	오빠/형
친구	결혼	고모/이모	남동생
태어났어요	이혼했어요	사촌/외사촌	언니/누나
죽었어요/ 돌아가셨어요	이혼	할아버지/ 외할아버지	여동생
결혼해요	총각	할머니/ 할머니	아들

(4) personality, character	(4) funny	(4) weak	(4) afraid (of)
(4) characteristic	(4) distressing	(4) angry	(4) joyful
(4) feelings	(4) exciting	(4) shy	(4) very
(4) temperament	(4) amazing	(4) generous	(4) a little
(4) (good) manners	(4) different	(4) miserly	(4) completely
(4) nice	(4) similar	(4) clever	(4) to believe
(4) happy	(4) strange	(4) stupid	(4) to think
(4) sad	(4) normal, usual	(4) lazy	(4) to like
(4) truthful	(4) boring	(4) energetic	(4) to dislike, to hate
(4) sorry	(4) strong	(4) well-behaved	(4) to feel

두려워해요	약해요	웃겨요	성격
즐거워요	화났어요	괴로워요	개성
매우, 아주	수줍워요	흥미로워요	감정
조금	관대해요	놀라워요	성질
완전히	인색해요	달라요	매너 있어요
믿다	똑똑해요	비슷해요	좋아요
생각하다	멍청해요	이상해요	행복해요
좋아하다	게을러요	늘 마찬가지예요	슬퍼요
싫어하다	활동적이에요	지루해요	진실해요
느끼다	착해요	튼튼해요	유감스러워요

⑤ store	⑤ expensive	⑤ wallet	⑤ few, a little
⑤ shop	⑤ offer	⑤ bag	⑤ many, much
⑤ open	⑤ clerk	⑤ sack, large bag	⑤ account, bill
⑤ closed	⑤ merchant	⑤ copper	⑤ receipt
⑤ market	⑤ bakery	⑤ silver	⑤ reduction, sale
⑤ shopping center	⑤ butcher	⑤ gold	⑤ to pay
⑤ price	⑤ fish seller	⑤ leather	⑤ to buy
⑤ cash (money)	⑤ grocer	⑤ wood	⑤ to give
⑤ money	⑤ tailor	⑤ free (of charge)	⑤ to cost
⑤ cheap	⑤ jeweler	⑤ gift	⑤ it is found, located

조금	지갑	비싸다	상점
많이	가방	할인판매	가게
계산서	베낭	점원	열어요
영수증	구리	상인	닫아요
세일	은	제과점	시장
지불하다	금	정육점	쇼핑센터
사다	가죽	생선가게	가격
주다	목재	식료품점	현금
들다	공짜	재단사	돈
...에 있다	선물	보석상	싸다

(6) clothes	(6) dress	(6) bathrobe	(6) green (colored)
(6) fashion	(6) skirt	(6) cloth, textile	(6) brown (colored)
(6) underwear	(6) blouse	(6) wool	(6) orange (colored)
(6) size	(6) coat	(6) cotton	(6) pink (colored)
(6) shirt	(6) waistcoat	(6) silk	(6) purple (colored)
(6) pants, trousers	(6) glove	(6) black (colored)	(6) light (colored)
(6) shoe	(6) sock	(6) red (colored)	(6) dark, deep (colored)
(6) sandal	(6) hat	(6) yellow (colored)	(6) comfortable
(6) jacket	(6) belt	(6) blue (colored)	(6) to wear, to put on
(6) suit	(6) jeans	(6) white (colored)	(6) to take off

녹(색)	드레싱 가운	드레스	옷
갈(색)	천	치마	패션
주황(색)	모직	브라우스	속옷
분홍(색)	면	코트	사이즈
보라(색)	비단	조끼	셔츠
연한(색)	검정(색)	장갑	바지
진한(색)	빨강(색)	양말	신발
편안하다	노랑(색)	모자	샌달
입다	파랑(색)	혁대	자켓
벗다	흰(색)	청바지	정장

food ⑦	oil ⑦	fruit ⑦	bananas ⑦
menu ⑦	cheese ⑦	salad ⑦	milk ⑦
dish ⑦	eggs ⑦	soy sauce ⑦	juice ⑦
meal ⑦	meat ⑦	onions ⑦	water ⑦
sugar ⑦	lamb, mutton ⑦	potatoes ⑦	coffee ⑦
butter ⑦	beef ⑦	carrots ⑦	tea ⑦
salt ⑦	pork ⑦	grapes ⑦	alcohol ⑦
pepper ⑦	chicken ⑦	apples ⑦	dessert, sweet ⑦
bread ⑦	fish ⑦	oranges ⑦	to eat ⑦
cooked rice ⑦	vegetables ⑦	lemons ⑦	to drink ⑦

바나나	과일	기름	음식
우유	샐러드	치즈	메뉴
주스	간장	달걀	반찬
물	양파	고기	식사
커피	감자	양고기	설탕
차	당근	소고기	버터
술	포도	돼지고기	소금
후식	사과	닭고기	후추
먹다	오렌지	생선	빵
마시다	레몬	채소	밥

body ⑧	belly, stomach ⑧	finger ⑧	lip ⑧
skeleton ⑧	arm ⑧	toe ⑧	bone ⑧
head ⑧	leg ⑧	thumb ⑧	skin ⑧
face ⑧	foot ⑧	chest ⑧	to see ⑧
eye ⑧	knee ⑧	back ⑧	to hear ⑧
ear ⑧	hand ⑧	heart ⑧	to smell ⑧
nose ⑧	elbow ⑧	hair ⑧	to taste ⑧
mouth ⑧	wrist ⑧	brain ⑧	to touch ⑧
tongue ⑧	shoulder ⑧	blood ⑧	to move *(something)* ⑧
neck ⑧	tooth ⑧	lung ⑧	to move *(yourself)* ⑧

입술	손가락	배	몸
뼈	발가락	팔	해골
피부	엄지손가락	다리	머리
보다	가슴	발	얼굴
듣다	등	무릎	눈
냄새 맡다	심장	손	귀
맛보다	머리/ 머리카락	팔꿈치	코
만지다	뇌	손목	입
옮기다	피	어깨	혀
움직이다	폐	이빨	목

health (9)	pulse (9)	accident (9)	addicted (to) (9)
healthy (9)	headache (9)	hospital (9)	smoking (9)
illness (9)	injury (9)	doctor (9)	diet (9)
patient (noun) (9)	wound (9)	nurse (9)	to suffer (from) (9)
cold (9)	pain (9)	ambulance (9)	to take (medicine, etc.) (9)
to catch a cold (9)	painful (9)	operation, surgery (9)	to fall (9)
sick (9)	medicine (9)	burn (9)	to break (9)
fever (9)	pill, tablet (9)	cure, treatment (9)	to cough (9)
diarrhea (9)	prescription (9)	first aid (9)	to swallow (9)
cough (9)	thermometer (9)	habit (9)	to smoke (9)

중독되다	사고	맥박	건강
흡연	병원	두통	건강하다
다이어트	의사	부상	병
고통을 받다	간호사	상처	환자
먹다	구급차	고통	감기
넘어지다	수술	고통스럽다	감기 걸리다
부러지다	화상	약	아프다
기침하다	치료	알약	열
삼키다	응급 치료	처방전	설사
담배피우다	습관	체온계	기침

hobby (10)	basketball (10)	singing, song (10)	reading (10)
spare time (10)	volleyball (10)	group, band (10)	cinema (10)
sports (10)	tennis (10)	singer (10)	play (theater) (10)
athletic (10)	Taekwondo (10)	musical instrument (10)	drawing (10)
game (10)	Korean wrestling (10)	flute (10)	photography (10)
player (10)	running, jogging (10)	violin (10)	hunting (10)
team (10)	skiing (10)	guitar (10)	fishing (10)
training (10)	swimming (10)	piano (10)	to play (a sport) (10)
coach (10)	dancing (10)	trumpet (10)	to play (strings, percussion/ wind, brass) (10)
soccer, football (10)	music (10)	drum (10)	to be interested in (10)

책읽기	노래	농구	취미
영화관	그룹	배구	여가 시간
연극	가수	테니스	운동
그림 그리기	악기	태권도	스포티한
사진술	플루트	씨름	게임
사냥	바이올린	달리기	선수
낚시	기타	스키	팀
하다	피아노	수영	훈련
치다/불다	트럼펫	춤	코치
관심있다	드럼	음악	축구

media	press	file	director
communication	news	Internet	producer
technology	newspaper	website	correspondent
broadcast, broadcasting	magazine	channel	photographer
television	article	telephone	broadcaster, announcer
radio	computer	cell phone, mobile phone	to watch
sound	keyboard	advertisement	to listen
tape	screen	program	to record
disc	printer	journalist	to print
recorder	scanner	editor	to publish

감독	파일	출판물	대중매체
프로듀서	인터넷	뉴스	통신
통신	웹사이트	신문	기술
사진사	채널	잡지	방송
아나운서	전화기	논설	텔레비전
보다	휴대폰	컴퓨터	라디오
듣다	광고	키보드	음향
녹음하다	프로그램	스크린	테이프
복사하다	기자	프린터	디스크
출판하다	편집자	스캐너	녹음기

(12) weather	(12) heat	(12) rain	(12) water
(12) environment	(12) hot	(12) snow	(12) air
(12) nature	(12) clear, fine	(12) snowy	(12) earth, dust
(12) atmosphere, weather	(12) temperature	(12) sunny	(12) fire
(12) climate	(12) cold (noun)	(12) cloudy	(12) wind
(12) season	(12) cold (adjective)	(12) rainy	(12) storm
(12) spring	(12) warm	(12) sky	(12) pollution
(12) summer	(12) moderate, temperate	(12) earth, land	(12) cause, reason
(12) autumn	(12) humidity	(12) sun	(12) to cause
(12) winter	(12) cloud	(12) moon	(12) to protect

물	비	열	날씨
공기	눈	덥다	환경
흙	눈이 내리다	맑다	자연
불	화창하다	온도, 기온	대기
바람	구름이 끼다	추위	기후
폭풍	비가 내리다	춥다	계절
공해	하늘	따뜻하다	봄
이유	땅	적당하다	여름
초래하다	해, 태양	습도	가을
보호하다	달	구름	겨울

region (13)	complex (13) *(offices, apartments, etc.)*	temple (13)	farm (13)
place (13)	school (13)	church (13)	mountain (13)
city (13)	hotel (13)	library (13)	beach (13)
countryside (13)	restaurant (13)	zoo (13)	river (13)
village (13)	pharmacy (13)	pagoda (13)	north (13)
district, quarter (13)	bank (13)	museum (13)	west (13)
street, road, way (13)	park (13)	post office (13)	south (13)
traffic (13)	police station (13)	movie theater (13)	east (13)
congestion (13)	gas station (13)	theater (13)	to park (13) *(a vehicle)*
downtown (13)	palace (13)	bridge (13)	to get lost (13)

농장	신전, 절	단지	지역
산	교회	학교	장소
해변	도서관	호텔	도시
강	동물원	식당	시골
북쪽	탑	약국	마을
서쪽	박물관	은행	구
남쪽	우체국	공원	길
동쪽	영화관	경찰서	교통
주차하다	극장	주유소	체증
길을 잃다	다리	궁전	시내

travel, journey, trip (14)	boat (14)	one-way (14)	abroad (14)
tourism (14)	ship (14)	roundtrip (ticket) (14)	before (14)
visit (14)	bus (14)	sea (14)	after (14)
country (14)	airport (14)	seaside (14)	to go (14)
traveler (14)	bus stop (14)	baggage (14)	to walk (14)
car (14)	station (14)	camera (14)	to return (14)
taxi (14)	port, harbor (14)	postcard (14)	to travel (14)
bicycle (14)	passport (14)	fast (14)	to ride, to catch, to board (14)
train (14)	visa (14)	slow (14)	to spend (time) (14)
plane (14)	ticket (14)	straight on (14)	to arrive (14)

해외	편도	보트	여행
전	왕복표	배	관광
후	바다	버스	방문하다
가다	바닷가	공항	나라
걷다	짐	버스 정류장	여행객
돌아오다	카메라	역	자동차
여행가다	엽서	항구	택시
타다	빠르다	여권	자전거
쓰다	느리다	비자	기차
도착하다	바로	표	비행기

student, pupil (15)	semester, term (15)	notebook (15)	Korean language (15)
teacher (15)	lesson (15)	dictionary (15)	history (15)
professor (15)	homework (15)	letter (15) *(of the alphabet)*	geography (15)
elementary school (15)	book (15)	number (15)	science (15)
middle school (15)	exercise book (15)	question (15)	biology (15)
high school (15)	pen (15)	answer (15)	chemistry (15)
faculty (15)	pencil (15)	exam (15)	physics (15)
university, college (15)	eraser (15)	mathematics (15)	to study (15)
academy (15)	pencil sharpener (15)	literature (15)	to teach (15)
class, classroom (15)	ruler (15)	English language (15)	to learn (15)

한국어	공책	학기	학생
역사	사전	수업	교사, 선생님
지리	문자	숙제	교수
과학	번호	책	초등학교
생물학	질문	연습장	중학교
화학	답	펜	고등학교
물리학	시험	연필	학부
공부하다	수학	지우개	대학교
가르치다	문학	연필깎기	학원
배우다	영어	자	교실

(16) work	(16) worker, employee	(16) judge	(16) florist
(16) job, position	(16) businessman/ businesswoman	(16) engineer	(16) farmer
(16) profession	(16) secretary	(16) mechanic	(16) artist
(16) company	(16) employee	(16) pilot	(16) unemployment
(16) branch	(16) civil servant	(16) driver	(16) unemployed
(16) office	(16) expert	(16) electrician	(16) retirement
(16) experience	(16) researcher	(16) plumber	(16) retired
(16) trade	(16) doctor	(16) cook	(16) salary
(16) employer, boss	(16) trader	(16) scientist	(16) to work
(16) manager, director	(16) lawyer	(16) barber	(16) to employ

꽃장수	판사	직원	일
농부	엔지니어	사업가	직업
예술가	기계공	비서	전문 직업
실업	조종사	근로자	회사
실업자	운전사	공무원	지사
퇴직	전기공	전문가	사무실
퇴직하다	배관공	연구원	경험
월급	요리사	의사	무역
일하다	과학자	무역업자	고용주
고용하다	이발사	변호사	관리자